'Knock Knock' Who's There?

The Truth About Jehovah's Witnesses

Anthony James

Copyright © 2013 Anthony James

All rights reserved.

ISBN: 147521765X

ISBN-13: 978-1475217650

Edited by E. Ledwood

To all those who helped me to think for myself

CONTENTS

	Acknowledgments	Pg 7
	Foreword By Jake Miller	Pg 9
1	The Witness View	Pg 11
2	Life As A Witness – My Early Years	Pg 33
3	Life As A Witness – Adulthood	Pg 51
4	Life As A Witness – My Escape	Pg 71
5	The History Lesson – 1799 ~ Present	Pg 97
6	The Dark Side – A Cult Following	Pg 121
7	A Concept Falls Apart	Pg 144
8	Conclusion	Pg 167
	Appendix	Pg 172
	Recommended Reading	Pg 184
	References	Pg 185

ACKNOWLEDGMENTS

The one who gave me so much support and encouragement as I undertook this project: my loving partner, Imogen. Without her I could not have made it as far as I have.

The ones that gave me an education in science and rational, critical thinking: Richard Dawkins, Christopher Hitchens, PZ Myers, Sam Harris, Jerry Coyne, Lawrence Krauss.

My partner in freedom: Jake.

My thanks also go to the few that gave me encouragement and support during the writing process, you know who you are ;)

DISCLAIMER

THE CONTENTS OF THIS BOOK ARE THE OPINION OF THE AUTHOR BASED ON PERSONAL EXPERIENCE AND THOROUGH RESEARCH. HE HAS MADE AN EARNEST EFFORT TO RELAY ONLY ACCURATE INFORMATION AND HAS PROVIDED QUOTES AND REFERENECES TO BACK UP HIS VIEWS. PLEASE NOTE: HE IS NOT EXEMPT FROM ERROR AND APOLOGISES FOR ANY MADE.

THE PURPOSE OF THIS BOOK

This book is designed to help anyone who is, has been, or knows someone who is a Jehovah's Witness. It also would likely be of interest to anyone who is interested in religious cults or someone who wants to know more about those people who come knocking.

It is my hope that the information within this book will help those who are struggling to break free from the grip of this religion. Information is power, and it is with sincerity that I provide what I hope is the armamentarium required to accomplish what every person is entitled to, namely freedom.

HOW TO USE THIS BOOK

The first chapter outlines and explains the fundamental beliefs of Jehovah's Witnesses. Chapters two to four tell my story as I grew up as a Witness. Chapter five breaks down the history of the religion with many aspects that are unknown to most Witnesses. Chapters six and seven pulls apart the religion and exposes many failings and fallacies that helped me to release the chains that wrapped and warped my mind.

By all means read some or all of this book in any order you wish. It is for your benefit, so use it as you wish, and share it with whomever you choose.

FOREWORD
BY JAKE MILLER

Unfortunately the exact time and date when I first met Anthony has eluded me. I do however remember the circumstances that surrounded our meeting. My friendship with Anthony started with a single text message shortly after the untimely passing of his father. Up until that point we didn't really have a friendship. The only reason we were even in the same place occasionally was because we were both under the reign of the tyrannical Jehovah's Witness Corporation. Anthony had been warned against associating with me because of my somewhat reckless approach to the religion. We were more like ships passing in the night sharing a friendly hello and a forced "brotherly" smile. When I heard Anthony's terrible news I felt obliged to send him a message expressing my sadness for his loss and to offer the only thing I did best, a session in a pub. Anthony agreed and a time was set. Ironically the time set was immediately after a meeting. Suited and booted, we converged on our local drinking establishment to drown his sorrows and to reminisce about the good times he had spent with his father. From this point onwards our friendship grew. At the beginning neither of us knew how vital we would be to each other in the future.

I like to think that I helped Anthony through the difficult parts of his life and I know he proved to be a rock for me in the very difficult time that I had ahead of me. Between us we have had much more then our fair share of heartache. We've battled through the passing away of loved ones, a religion that would have seen us broken men had we not escaped, numerous medical disasters (and more than one relationship disaster) and we are both still battling against some very severe depression. Without each other I know that I would not be here to write this foreword and I can honestly say that I'm so glad I've got the opportunity. When Anthony first told me he was going to write a book about the religion that clouded a large part of our lives, I was very excited. One of the main reasons that I was excited was because I knew how determined Anthony could be when he believed in something so strongly. I can safely say that not only do I believe in this book and that the contents could both save and inspire "great crowds" of people, I also believe in Anthony James. He is a strong, accomplished man and I am forever thankful to have been a part of his journey leading up to this masterpiece. So grab a cup of tea and get comfortable because this is going to be one hell of a ride!

CHAPTER 1

THE WITNESS VIEW

With each day that passes as one of Jehovah's Witnesses, the world is in a state of accelerating decline. The great day of God draws closer and closer. God's judgement day will bring blessings for a small group of loyal followers and total merciless destruction for the rest of mankind. The whole world is under the Devil's control; He is driving it into the ground and trying to take us with it. We must, as instructed by our religious leadership, remain separate from the 'people of the world', despite living amongst them. We are different; a special chosen people serving the one true God under his only chosen organisation. Those who do not share our faith should not be held as close friends and we should limit our association with them. After all, they are part of Satan's 'system of things' and can draw us away from serving the one true God. The rest of the world's religions are corrupt products of Satan and his army of demons that oppose pure worship. Death will result for all who follow them. Thank goodness we came to know 'the truth' about the universal creator and his plan to redeem mankind... well, us Witnesses anyway.

We cannot just sit back and wait for this time. Our individual salvation depends on more than just having faith in God. We must recognise the need to spread the *news of God's plan for the world and recruit new members to help our cause and in turn, save their lives as well as our own. In the Western world we tend to meet mostly apathy as we go from door to door with our message. Try as we might to urge them to listen to our prophetic message, they just don't seem to want to know. What's more, they are annoyed that we keep calling. Why don't they see the bigger picture? Are they just selfish? Possibly, but we must remember that 'the whole world is lying in the power of the wicked one' as the bible states. The Devil rules the wicked system that these people are a part of and has blinded them so that they cannot see the truth of our message. If they don't turn to our beliefs before the end, their doom is inevitable.*

This is the fundamental outlook of the world that is so prevalent in the minds of each and every loyal Jehovah's Witness. You may be most familiar with them as they come to your door, smartly dressed and presenting their freshly printed copies of *The Watchtower* and *Awake!* magazines while you are attempting to decide whether to have toast or cereal on a Saturday morning. It might sound strange, yet this is really how Jehovah's Witnesses view things, and if you were to listen to them on your doorstep they will tell you just how urgent their message is because judgement day is so close. There are many tactics that are employed to get your attention and keep you talking, but we'll come to those later on. First, I want to give you an accurate description of exactly what they believe and where possible, why they believe it.

Breakdown of Jehovah's Witness Beliefs

Firstly, Witnesses adopt the use of 'Jehovah' as God's name; it is something they hold dearly.

> "God gave himself a name that is full of meaning. His name, Jehovah, means that God can fulfill any promise he makes and can carry out any purpose he has in mind." - *What Does The Bible Really Teach?* p.14.

They feel that by using God's name (although he has more than one, Yahweh for example) they are a more true religion than all the others. Many Bible translations have elected to use the word LORD instead of inserting the name of God. This is shameful according to Witnesses, who have their own Bible translation called 'The New World Translation of the Holy Scriptures' (NWT). It has both the old and new testament and uses Jehovah as God's name throughout.

> "Hence, the leaders both of Judaism and of Christendom share the blame for the widespread ignorance concerning the greatest name." - *The Greatest Name.*

This I hold as one of the many subtle yet powerful ways individuals are made to feel they are part of a special group. As largely they are taught that no other religion uses the true name of God, hence they are part of God's chosen organisation. Only such ones will be saved at Armageddon.

> "Very soon, Jehovah and Christ Jesus will execute judgment, and the cry will be heard: "The great day of their wrath has come, and who is able to stand?" (Revelation 6:17) The answer? Only a minority of mankind, including any of the sealed 144,000 who might still be remaining in the flesh and a great crowd of other sheep who will "stand," that is, survive with them. —Jeremiah 35:19; 1 Corinthians 16:13." - *Revelation, Its Grand Climax at Hand,* p.128.

The name Jehovah's Witnesses is derived from the scripture Isaiah 43 verse 10 where it reads: " 'YOU are my witnesses,' is the utterance of Jehovah..." (NWT). They do however, seem to fail to address the criticism by biblical scholars that in the New Testament the New World Translation renders the Greek word 'kyrios' as Jehovah when its literal translation is 'lord' or 'master'. Kyrious appears 237 times in the New Testament. Witnesses make a point of saying they will happily use any translation to prove their beliefs. They quite literally religiously use the

NWT when studying and only occasionally bring out another translation when it supports their own.

Jesus & The Trinity

Jehovah's Witnesses believe that Jesus Christ is the Son of God, his first creation who was known as Michael the Archangel whilst in heaven. Jehovah's Witnesses thereby reject the idea of the Trinity (Three gods making up the one Almighty God) and believe that by means of his sacrificial death, mankind can be forgiven of their errors and restored to the original 'paradise conditions' that we started with in the Garden of Eden.

> "All those future blessings, including life everlasting in perfect health, are made possible because Jesus died for us. To receive those blessings, we need to show that we appreciate the gift of the ransom." - *What Does The Bible Really Teach?* p.54.

Jesus' example as a perfect man has shown that being loyal to God is possible where Adam failed, Jesus succeeded, proving that it can be done. The Devil tried his best to break Jesus' integrity and cause him to falter. By his fine example, we have a role model to follow and therefore give ourselves the best chance of survival through to the promised paradise Earth (often called the 'New System'). According to Witness beliefs, Jesus was crowned as king in heaven in 1914. He immediately began to cleanse heaven of Satan and his demons by hurling them to the Earth. 1914 is a key date in Watchtower beliefs, with followers regarding the eruption of World War I as supporting evidence.

> "This...was completely fulfilled in 1914, when Jesus was installed as King of God's Kingdom and the time of the end began." - *Revelation, Its Grand Climax Now at Hand,* p.156.

Satan The Devil

He is the source of evil and the father of the lie. Satan is the fallen angel who became jealous of God's worship and sought the glory for himself. By deceiving both Adam and Eve into eating the forbidden fruit, he caused them to lose God's blessing, and consequently their perfection. He commands an army of demons who are also former angels. When these demons were banished to the Earth by Jesus (where they reside invisibly), they began causing worldwide havoc under Satan's control. Satan knows that he will be destroyed after Armageddon and therefore has no intention of doing anything other than causing chaos and agony for all of mankind, especially Jehovah's people.

> "The Devil uses his superhuman intelligence to launch treacherous and deadly strikes like those of a poisonous snake from a hidden place." - *The Watchtower*, 1st Oct 2007, p.26-30.

Since Jehovah's Witnesses are on the Earth, they are within his reach. His main aim is to turn as many faithful followers as he can away from God, in turn causing pain and suffering to God.

Why Does God Allow Suffering?

This is one of the most important questions in history, no doubt asked by those who believe during perhaps periods of doubt (like myself), or asked by a non-believer when questioning God's existence. I recall many an occasion when I have been asked: 'if there's a god, why does he allow all the suffering in the world?'. Naturally, Jehovah's Witnesses are prepared to answer such a question at your doorstep, so we'll break down their belief regarding this issue.

The first explanation is of course the fall of Adam and Eve from perfection into sin. This lost them God's favour and they became mortal. They began to die, the same as we do today, only a lot more slowly. Because they and many after them were 'so close to perfection' they had considerably longer lifespans than us today. Having produced children only after acquiring this new physical state, their children were also imperfect. As a result, every human in history from that point carried the same 'dent in the mould' and essentially are doomed, as the book *What Does The Bible Really Teach?* explains.

> "Adam and Eve rebelled against Jehovah. In effect, they said: "We do not need Jehovah as our Ruler. We can decide for ourselves what is right and what is wrong." How could Jehovah settle that issue? How could he teach all intelligent creatures that the rebels were wrong and that his way truly is best? Someone might say that God should simply have destroyed the rebels and made a fresh start. But Jehovah had stated his purpose to fill the earth with the offspring of Adam and Eve, and he wanted them to live in an earthly paradise. (Genesis 1:28) Jehovah always fulfills his purposes. (Isaiah 55:10, 11) Besides that, getting rid of the rebels in Eden would not have answered the question that had been raised regarding Jehovah's right to rule." - *What Does The Bible Really Teach?* p.109-110.

The book then goes on to give an illustration of a maths teacher trying to explain a difficult equation or problem. A rebellious student questions whether the teacher's method is the best solution and offers his own. The book reasons that the teacher *could* simply tell the student to be quiet. This would demonstrate the authority (power) of the teacher, but not address the issue raised. The book continues:

> "What should the teacher do? If he throws the rebels out of the class, what will be the effect on the other students? Will they not believe that their fellow student and those who joined him are right? All the other students in the class might lose respect for the teacher, thinking that he is afraid of being proved wrong. But suppose that the teacher allows the rebel to show the class how he would solve the problem." - *What Does The Bible Really Teach?* p.111.

The other students in the class are the remainder of God's angels in heaven. Despite neither being children nor imperfect, as in the analogy we are to accept that the angels couldn't use sound reasoning to determine whether or not God's way was right. This thought is unlikely to be considered by a Witness, the reasons for which will be discussed later. The book continues:

> "So, what has Jehovah done? He has allowed Satan to show how he would rule mankind. God has also allowed humans to govern themselves under Satan's guidance...Jehovah knows that all honesthearted humans and angels will benefit from seeing that Satan and his fellow rebels have failed and that humans cannot govern themselves." - *What Does The Bible Really Teach?* p.111.

This statement appears to be a straight contradiction. It says that Satan is ruling mankind and mankind is ruling itself with Satan's guidance. They can't both be true, unless Satan's way of ruling mankind is to let mankind rule himself, which whilst makes sense, is not clearly defined as being the case. Precisely how or why a human would benefit from life as an imperfect being in a world with suffering, pain, misery, and death only to see Satan and Man fail is not obvious to me. I must stress that this thought only occurred to me once I had distanced myself from the Witnesses and began to think for myself. For most of my life this reasoning seemed to make perfect sense, especially when I was surrounded by like minded people along with consuming an endless flow of literature produced by The Watchtower Society telling me how much sense it made.

The book next addresses the reason for the length of time God has permitted this suffering:

> "...he has not stopped Satan and those who side with him from trying to prove that they are right. Allowing time to pass has thus been necessary...injustice, poverty, crime, and war have grown

ever worse. Human rule has now been shown to be a failure." - *What Does The Bible Really Teach?* p.112.

Witnesses are constantly being told how the world is getting worse and society is on the brink of collapse. The book justifies God's decision to permit this wickedness by saying he will fix it later:

> "What, though, about all the harm that has been done during the long rebellion against God? We do well to remember that Jehovah is almighty. Therefore, he can and will undo the effects of mankind's suffering. - *What Does The Bible Really Teach?* p.112.

Another interesting point that never occurred to me until I had left the religion is that God had already very early on stepped in and caused a global flood, killing everything on the planet except what was in the ark with Noah and his family. That wasn't allowing Satan/Man to rule himself as had previously been explained. In the classroom analogy, it's as if half way through the student's workings on the blackboard the teacher decides to erase everything the student had done, out of the blue and for no apparent reason. That thought aside, we move on to the second justification for the allowance of suffering, Job.

Witnesses are told that the when Satan approached Jehovah God and questioned Job's integrity, the challenge applies to all humans.

> "Satan questioned Job's motive for serving God. The Devil said to Jehovah: "Have not you yourself put up a hedge about [Job] and about his house and about everything that he has all around? ...Satan thus argued that Job served God just for what he got in return. The Devil also charged that if Job was tested, he would turn against God. How did Jehovah respond to Satan's challenge? Since the issue involved Job's motive, Jehovah allowed Satan to test Job. In this way, Job's love for God—or lack of it—would be clearly shown." - *What Does The Bible Really Teach?* p.117.

I thought Satan had already been granted rule of the Earth, but here it seems God has given him special permission to inflict misery on Job. Nevertheless, the book explains:

> "The issue of integrity to God that was raised by Satan was not directed against Job alone. You too are involved... Satan made it clear that his charge applied not just to Job but to all humans. That is a very important point. Satan has called into question your integrity to God." - *What Does The Bible Really Teach?* p.119-120.

The required number of examples of individuals who pass the tests from Satan by living a life of faithful service to God is not given. We have to wait patiently and be watchful for the tests, and they may come from unexpected sources:

> "Satan's influence may be seen when friends, relatives, or others oppose your efforts to study the Bible..." - *What Does The Bible Really Teach?* p.120.

This belief is part of a system of control that instils in the individual an emotional trigger of fear, which will be discussed in chapter six.

One True Religion vs. Babylon the Great

Like quite a few religious groups, Witnesses believe they are the only religion that teaches 'The Truth' and therefore the only means of salvation. All other religions are part of what the bible calls 'Babylon the Great'. They believe that this is the 'world empire of false religion', which is every religion except Jehovah's Witnesses. Owned and operated by the Devil, this 'Babylon the Great' is described as a 'harlot' who remorselessly misleads mankind and is guilty of spilling the blood of countless millions throughout history. She is a harlot because of her wilful involvement with politics and war. By supporting wars of governments on both sides and encouraging their followers to go to war for God and country "they have committed fornication with the kings of the Earth".

The Witnesses tend to focus on the positive side of God's promise to restore peace, rather than catastrophic levels of death that are to precede it. It makes sense since they are expecting to be spared Jehovah's wrath and fury; it's everyone else who'll be facing judgement. Or so they hope.

> "The Bible teaches that God will soon bring an end to this wicked system of things and will replace it with a righteous new world under the rulership of his Kingdom. (2 Peter 3:9, 13) What a marvellous world that will be! And in that righteous new system, there will be only one religion, one true form of worship. Is it not the course of wisdom for you to take the necessary steps to come into association with true worshipers right now?" - *What Does The Bible Really Teach?* p.153.

As Witnesses believe they are the only true religion, they refer to their beliefs as 'The Truth'. This expression is probably used at least once daily by every one of them. This curious phrase will be analysed later.

Heaven, Angels, and the Anointed Class

There are untold numbers of existing angels in heaven. A select few humans who are loyal servants of God (Jehovah's Witnesses) will not get to go to the Earthly paradise, but will live eternally in Heaven as 'kings and priests'. These are the 'Anointed Class' and number 144,000 individuals. How does a Jehovah's Witness know if he or she is of the Anointed? Apparently God's Holy Spirit tells them so, usually when they get baptised.

Jehovah apparently started choosing these individuals just after the time of Jesus (Penticost 33CE) and this carries through to present day. 144,000 is a very small number, especially considering how many loyal Christians must have lived in the two thousand or so years since Jesus' day.

> "For 19 centuries there was only the one calling, the heavenly one, with Jehovah being very selective as to who would serve with his Son to make up the Kingdom government. Many would be invited but only a precious few chosen. (Matthew 22:2, 14) In time the prescribed but limited number of 144,000 would be reached. After this no more would be anointed by holy spirit as witness that they had the heavenly hope, unless, in a rare occurrence, the unfaithfulness of one of the remaining 'chosen ones' made a replacement necessary." - *The Watchtower,* Feb 15th 1982, p.30.

Currently there are believed to be over eleven thousand members of the 144,000 anointed still alive today. Strangely this number has been growing over the last few years. When I was growing up the number of anointed still alive was around eight thousand. Why is this significant?

> "Logically, the calling of the little flock would draw to a close when the number was nearing completion, and the evidence is that the general gathering of these specially blessed ones ended in 1935." - *The Watchtower,* Feb 15th 1995, p.19.

If the period for choosing anointed ones to go to heaven had ended in 1935, we would expect to see the number decreasing as they become elderly and pass away.

> "...the number of genuine anointed disciples of Christ is dwindling, though some will evidently still be on earth when the great tribulation begins. Most of the remnant are quite elderly, and over the years the number of those who are <u>truly anointed</u> has been getting smaller." - *The Watchtower,* Jan 15th 2000, p.13.

Truly anointed? It would seem that The Watchtower Society are trying to subtly explain this perhaps embarrassing reality of increase in membership of the anointed class by implying that some are making this claim falsely. It would be unlikely that as we draw to the apparent brink of Armageddon, God would suddenly remember he needs 3000 or more replacements to fill this prophetic heavenly number. Would he be running the risk of 'scraping the bottom of the barrel' by leaving it this late. Does he have to hastily choose these ones to fill his quota?

The Faithful and Discreet Slave

This is the name given to the leadership of Jehovah's Witnesses. The problem with this teaching is that the 'Anointed Class' are the 'Faithful and Discreet Slave'. However, those who profess to be of this class have no say at all in any aspect of any of the religion's beliefs, policies, doctrines or teachings. Only members of the 'Governing Body' in New York, (currently only eight men as women have no place in congregational leadership according to Witness beliefs) set the rules, regulations and teachings. They review and edit the work of the 'Writing Department' (mostly comprised of non-anointed Witnesses), which is published in their books and magazines. These are distributed to the congregations globally as 'Spiritual Food'. Individuals of the Governing Body are members of the Anointed Class and until recently claimed to be the spokesman for the rest of 144,000. In 2012 at the Annual Meeting, it was announced that the term 'Faithful and Discreet Slave' now refers to the Governing Body only, and not the 144,000.

> "The faithful and discreet slave" was appointed over Jesus' domestics in 1919. That slave is the small, composite group of anointed brothers serving at world headquarters during Christ's presence who are directly involved in preparing and dispensing spiritual food. When this group work together as the Governing Body, they act as "the faithful and discreet slave." - *Jehovah's Witnesses Annual Report 2012*.

Great Crowd of Other Sheep

In 1935 the Watchtower President Joseph Rutherford declared that salvation would not only be available to the 144,000 anointed ones, but also to a 'Great Crowd of Other Sheep'. These would be faithful

Witnesses who don't possess the heavenly hope; rather they will live on paradise Earth forever. Hence from 1935 onwards the preaching work exploded as a 'great gathering work' and the organisation grew, with most new members having the 'Earthly Hope'.

> "Since 1935 a growing great crowd of other sheep has heard their triumphant song and been moved to join with them in publicizing God's Kingdom." - *Revelation, Its Grand Climax at Hand*, p.201.

The Great Tribulation

Jehovah's Witnesses feel we are so close to this fearful time that they can almost touch it. The great tribulation is said to be a time of worldwide anarchy where the last form of government is to be tried, a global government. The United Nations is taught to be the totalitarian instigator of this arrangement. Once a worldwide dictatorial regime is in place, it will start to destroy all religion in the world in favour of a worldwide single religion. Jehovah's Witnesses being the single, true religion will be the last one standing. As soon as the UN makes its strike against God's people, He will react as if his eyeball had been touched. The battle of Armageddon will immediately begin.

> "There are billions of people who do not know Jehovah. Many of them in ignorance practice things that God's Word shows to be wicked. If they persist in this course, they will be among those who perish during the great tribulation." - *The Watchtower*, Oct 1st 1993, p.19.

Where elements of fear develop here is perhaps two-fold. The duration of the 'Great Tribulation' is not known, so how long faithful witnesses will have to endure this prophetic time of untold trouble can be a cause of apprehension. Added to this is the fact that salvation is not guaranteed to anyone. Despite the teaching that forgiveness is by God's 'Grace' or 'Underserved Kindness', the contradicting teaching that faith without works is dead. A witness must therefore demonstrate his faith by performing the works as set out by the 'Faithful and Discreet Slave' (The Watchtower Society's Governing Body) to the best of his ability wherever and as often as he can.

> "A person does not earn salvation by his works. But anyone who has genuine faith will have works go with it – works of obedience to the commands of God and Christ, works that demonstrate his faith and love. Without such works, his faith is dead." - *Reasoning from the Scriptures*, p.359.

Armageddon

It is the day that strikes fear to countless religious people throughout the world. Jehovah's Witnesses being no exception, religious people strongly believe that this day of war and judgement is imminent; they are therefore desperately spreading the message via the door-to-door and other preaching methods. Why are many individuals secretly afraid of this day? Salvation is not guaranteed to anyone, including baptised Witnesses. All must face the judgement and if deemed acceptable by God will be rewarded with eternal life on a paradise Earth (with a couple of clauses attached). Those who are deemed unrighteous will face the 'Lake of Fire and Sulphur' and be destroyed forever. Most of the world's living population will be destroyed according to teachings of the Watchtower; this is why the preaching work is so important. Satan will be bound and hurled into the Abyss for a thousand years.

> "Only Jehovah's Witnesses, those of the anointed remnant and the "great crowd," as a united organization under the protection of the Supreme Organizer, have any Scriptural hope of surviving the impending end of this doomed system dominated by Satan the Devil." - *The Watchtower,* Sep 1st 1989, p.19.

The teachings go as far as to say God will also execute non-Jehovah's Witness children at Armageddon.

"What will happen to young children at Armageddon? The Bible does not directly answer that question, and we are not the judges. However, the Bible does show that God views the young children of true Christians as "holy." (1 Cor. 7:14) It also reveals that in times past when God destroyed the wicked he likewise destroyed their little ones." - *Reasoning from the Scriptures,* p.47-48.

Christ's Millennial Reign & The Resurrection

After Armageddon, Jesus will begin his millennial reign. During this literal one thousand years, Earth will be restored to a paradise, and all those who have died will be resurrected to eternal life in perfect bodies. Surviving humans will slowly be restored to bodily perfection; the old will grow young, the sick will return to health. Animals will reside with mankind in perfect peace and harmony.

> "...the millions of the great crowd who have now come out of the great tribulation stand conspicuously "before the throne." These have already been counted righteous for survival because of their faith in Jesus' shed blood, but their judging must continue through the thousand years as Jesus keeps on guiding them to "fountains of waters of life." Then, having been restored to human perfection and thereafter tested, they will be declared righteous in the fullest sense. (Revelation 7:9, 10, 14, 17) Children who survive the great tribulation and any children born to the great crowd during the Millennium will similarly need to be judged during the thousand years. —Compare Genesis 1:28; 9:7; 1 Corinthians 7:14. - *Revelation, Its Grand Climax at Hand,* p.296.

After Christ's Millennial Reign

As soon as the thousand years of peace has ended, Satan will be released from the Abyss and allowed a short period of time to try and turn as many people as he can away from God. As all people on Earth will now be perfect God will execute any who choose to follow Satan into wickedness as soon as the allotted time for testing is over, along with Satan and his demons.

> "By the end of the Thousand Year Reign, all earth will have come to resemble the original Eden. It will be a veritable paradise. Perfect mankind will no longer need a high priest to intercede for it before God, since all traces of Adamic sin will have been removed and the last enemy, death, brought to nothing. Christ's Kingdom will have achieved God's purpose to create one world with one government." - *Revelation, Its Grand Climax Now at Hand* p.291.

> "Now as soon as the thousand years have been ended, Satan will be let loose out of his prison, and he will go out to mislead those nations..." - Revelation 20:7.

Once his final effort is deemed finished by God, Satan will face immediate execution.

> "Rather than being merely abyssed, this time Satan, the original serpent, will actually be crushed out of existence, pulverized, completely annihilated as if by fire." - *Revelation, Its Grand Climax at Hand,* p.293.

The whole issue of fallen man, the Devil's rebellion and God's reputation will have been settled forever. The original plan will be back on track and any who choose to rebel in the future will face instant destruction by God. Those who remain obedient to God's commandments will enjoy eternal life on Earth in paradise conditions, with no death, disease, famine, crime or any other problems of any kind.

Requirements

There are a few requirements in order to receive the gift of God's 'undeserved kindness' and inherit a perfect body on paradise Earth with an eternal life, rich with happiness and fulfilment. You must repent of your sins, become a Jehovah's Witness by dedicating yourself to God (and perhaps unknowingly to the Watchtower Bible and Tract Society), attend their religious meetings as often as you possibly can (2-3 times per week), participate in the door-to-door preaching work as frequently as you're able and donate as much money as you feel you can to the organisation on a regular basis.

> "Jesus is watching the rich drop contributions into the temple treasury chest. In the crowd he notices a needy widow who donates **"two small coins** of very little value." (Luke 21:2) Jesus praises her act of generosity. Why? Because the others had donated "out of their surplus, but she, out of her want, dropped in all of what she had, her **whole living.**" — Mark 12:44.
>
> Do you have the same priorities as this woman did? Are you willing to spend your time and money in serving God? Like the needy widow, you can donate toward the **maintenance** of places of worship. You can also spend your time and money **helping others** learn about Jehovah God. Jehovah noticed and appreciated the small amount the widow gave in his service. God will also appreciate and help you if your **top priority** is to do his will." - *Questions Young People Ask: Volume 2,* p.166.

In addition to this you'll be required to complete and sign an Advanced Medical Directive stating your refusal of blood transfusions.

> "...the command to abstain from blood means that we would not allow anyone to transfuse blood into our veins." - *What Does The Bible Really Teach?* p.130.

In order to get baptised as one of Jehovah's Witnesses you'll need to have shown yourself to have made personal changes in your lifestyle to bring yourself in line with the standards set out by the Watchtower Society. These include maintaining a moral standard, free from sexual contact outside marriage (including masturbation), a commitment to honesty in all your dealings, earnest efforts to resist the use of 'foul language', and refusal to be involved in any kind of politics or military.

> "Jehovah's witnesses are according to God's Word no part of this world which is governed by the political systems. For this important Bible reason they tell officials of the government that they conscientiously object to serving in any military establishment or any civilian arrangement that substitutes for military service." - *The Watchtower*, Feb 1st 1951, p.77.

You are also to limit your social contact with non-witnesses as they are considered 'bad association'.

> "We must also be on guard against extended association with worldly people. Perhaps it is a neighbor, a school friend, a workmate, or a business associate." - *The Watchtower*, Feb 15th 1994, p.24.

You'll be required to carefully review and throw away any entertainment (be it books, films, or video games) that feature violence, the paranormal, or sexual content.

> "...much of what is available glorifies things that God hates, including violence, spiritism, and illicit sex. Therefore, you need to scrutinize the type of recreation and entertainment that you engage in. What effect does it have on you? Does it encourage in you a spirit of violence, fierce competition, or nationalism?" - *The Watchtower*, Jan 15th 2013.

Drug use, including tobacco is categorically forbidden, as is alcohol beyond moderate use.

Most of these requirements seem like pretty decent improvements one can make to their life, with the exception of examples of high control such as blood transfusions, association, entertainment and sexuality.

Women

The position towards women is perhaps of particular concern to those on the outside, whilst seemingly going completely unchallenged on the inside. Women Witnesses (referred to as 'sisters') are considered 'weaker vessels', and males (brothers) are viewed as their heads. Sisters are not allowed to take the lead in any congregational matters, including teaching, unless a baptised brother is not available.

> "The apostle Paul wrote: "I do not permit a woman... to exercise authority over a man, but to be in silence. For Adam was formed first, then Eve." (1 Timothy 2:12, 13) This does not mean that a woman is to be completely silent at a meeting of the Christian congregation. She is to be silent in the sense of not getting into disputes with a man. She is not to belittle his appointed position or endeavor to teach the congregation. Men have been given the assignment of presiding over and teaching the congregation, but women add much to Christian meetings by participating in them in various ways." - *The Watchtower*, Jan 15th 2007.

Wives must be submissive to their husbands and render their due (make themselves available for sex), without holding back. This attitude towards women is put across as a loving arrangement from God.

> "What can couples do to help them avoid being tempted to look outside the marriage for sexual satisfaction? The Bible states: "Let the husband render to his wife her due; but let the wife also do likewise to her husband.' " - *Awake!* Nov 2011.

On an occasion when a baptised male is not present and a prayer is required for a group of sisters, one may volunteer to offer the prayer. She must wear a head covering, be it a hat, scarf, or even a tea towel.

> "If a sister has to handle duties usually performed by a brother at a congregationally arranged meeting or meeting for field service,

she should wear a head covering." - *The Watchtower*, July 15th 2002, p.27.

Organisational & Congregational Structure

At the congregation level you have your 'brothers' and 'sisters' - regular baptised Jehovah's Witnesses. Some of these are also 'pioneers', who have committed around 50 – 70 hours each month to the preaching work. They do not receive any financial support for this, and therefore must also work to cover their housing, food and other expenses. Anointed brothers and sisters do not have any special privileges or hold any particular authority in the congregation. In effect, they are just normal brothers and sisters.

Certain brothers who are 'reaching out' will be granted the position of 'Ministerial Servant'. They will have more responsibilities and are required to support the leaders of the congregation, the 'Elders'. Depending on the size of the congregation, the number of Elders who form the 'Body of Elders' varies, although it is normally in the region of six to twelve men. Elders do not need to be members of the anointed, nor do they need to be pioneers. Each congregation will have a presiding overseer who handles certain matters.

There are also men who hold the position of 'Circuit Overseer'. They are assigned to work a certain area where they travel round the congregations. During their week-long stay, they offer encouragement and council to the regular Witnesses and the Elder Body. They are also there to advise the Elders how to handle any important or difficult issues that may have arisen. Circuit overseers receive a very small financial allowance and are granted the use of a Watchtower owned car whilst they are doing this work.

Many countries have a 'Regional Branch Office' called 'Bethel' (House of God). It is Bethel that handles the distribution of literature to the various congregations, oversees and organises them, and are the local contact for congregational Elders who need advice on important or unclear matters. The branch office ultimately reports all relevant information and the statistics for all data back to Watchtower headquarters in Brooklyn, New York. This includes each congregation's reported number of hours in the preaching work, the number of magazines left with householders, and the number of bible studies started with members of the public (as well as other statistics). Many of the Bethel facilities have large printing presses including Japan, Brazil, Britain, USA, Mexico, and South Africa, where publications are produced in multiple languages.

The headquarters is of course in New York, where numerous large buildings are occupied for the multiple organisational activities that the Watchtower Society undertakes. It is considered a great privilege to serve at any Bethel and applicants must have a high standard of conduct, cleanliness and reputation, as well as an excellent service record in the preaching work. It is strongly advised that individuals who apply are around the ages of 25 – 30 and are unmarried. They are given accommodation and food in exchange for unpaid labour. Many duties await volunteers, including working in the printing presses, cleaning, laundry and mechanics. They are also expected to maintain a strict personal bible study schedule and attend meetings at a local congregation, as well as full-time pioneer work (preaching for seventy hours per month).

At the top of the hierarchical structure we find the Governing Body. As previously mentioned it is made up of eight men who make all doctrinal and policy decisions for fellow Jehovah's Witnesses worldwide. Six assigned departmental committees support them. These are categorised as Personnel, Publishing, Service, Teaching, Writing and Coordinating. Each of these 'teams' implements the decisions of the Governing Body. Whilst it seems they don't each earn a personal fortune, they do live a luxurious lifestyle. What's more, they get to control the lives of over seven million people, by setting rules, regulations and policies that filter through to each congregation.

CHAPTER 2

LIFE AS A WITNESS

MY EARLY YEARS

I was born to a father who was raised as a Witness and mother who became one in her twenties. My memories of my early childhood are largely happy, growing up in a small cottage in a village about an hour away from my birthplace. I shared a room with my younger sister for the eleven years we lived there. My father worked very hard as a landscaper; my mother a part-time teacher. We lived within our means, never going hungry but by no means wealthy. Having acquired a near dustbin size bucket full of Lego, the only potential for feeling underprivileged would have been a lack of imagination, which luckily I did not have. With that huge tub of connectable bricks I could create any toy I wanted. The hours upon hours I spent making and breaking Lego structures filled my childhood with enjoyment, and no doubt kept me quiet.

It was not all smooth sailing as father was prone to a short and fierce temper. He never physically harmed us as children, aside from occasional use of a belt, hand, or wooden spoon for discipline, although his ability to become enraged (seemingly in an instant) made us quite afraid of him. It was hard to tell when you were in his good books, but you sure knew it when you were in his bad. We often had little clue as to why he was in such a foul mood, we just had to remain quiet and out of the way while he slammed doors and eventually went upstairs until he'd calmed down. The morning after any particularly unpleasant outbursts of rage, we may have been greeted with a hug and brief apology, which went at least some way to settling any resentment towards him.

Our mother was the good Christian wife, supportive to her husband but never outspoken as to disrespect him, publicly or at home. She played her role in the family to textbook Witness perfection. She would be much softer and more loving to us, perhaps overly so by way of compensation, but never speaking ill of our father. She was highly educated, capable of deep feeling and understanding, ready to offer sound advice to anyone who asked of her. She was also the one everyone wanted on their quiz team, as with her they'd probably win. She was not a pushover though, far from it, quite capable of putting her foot down when needed, which made her a respected teacher at primary school.

Of course the main part of our life was serving Jehovah God by being as busy as possible in 'Spiritual Activities', of which there were many. At the time we had two meetings at the Kingdom Hall on a Sunday morning, two on a Tuesday evening, and one on a Thursday evening. The Thursday night meeting was held at a local Brother's home where around ten of us would attend for an hour-long Bible based book study, or perhaps more accurately, a book based Bible study. We were required to look up the carefully chosen scriptures that were cited to support what the book said, as opposed to just reading the Bible and discussing what *that* says. Tuesday night's featured a double meeting comprised of an hour long 'Theocratic Ministry School', where we were trained to perform the door-to-door field service. This was followed by an hour long 'Service Meeting', which was similar in topic just considerably less interesting. We were to endure three or more talks, filling the time in such a monotonous and dreary way as to leave me praying for 9 O'clock to arrive, just so I could go home to bed.

The Sunday morning meeting was also held at the Kingdom Hall and consisted of an hour long 'Public Talk' followed by the mind numbingly tedious hour long 'Watchtower Study'. The public talks were usually quite enjoyable to listen to, though no audience participation was allowed. Surprisingly, it was *The Watchtower* study, which was based around audience participation that was the duller of the two. Probably the reason for this was that a paragraph would be read aloud, a question asked (questions were printed at the bottom of the article) and Brothers and Sisters would raise their hands to answer. Maybe three or four answers would be taken before the brother conducting the study would move on to the next paragraph, where the process would be repeated. Most of the time, the answers were repeated straight out of the paragraph that had just been read, with extra kudos going to anyone who offered any further points of interest. A factor adding to the boredom-fest that was this meeting was that everyone was supposed to study the article in advance. This took at least as long as the actual study (sometimes longer) as we'd go through the article, read a paragraph, ask the question and underline the answer within the paragraph, all in preparation for doing the same thing on the Sunday. Enduring this as an adult was bad enough, but as a child it was far more difficult. Despite believing everything being taught, it was a tall stretch to expect little ones to pay attention to material designed for adults for hours each week. We had to sit still, silently, without toys, a pen and pad to doodle, a colouring book, not even a children's book with the occasional exception of 'My Book of Bible Stories' to keep us engaged mentally. If we were to misbehave by whispering too loudly or getting restless, then a parent would take the offending child to the back room for a smack who would then be brought back in with the threat of further, worse smacking clearly in mind should they be trouble again. Don't for a second be fooled into thinking that this was just my family, no – it was, and still is the 'done thing'. Occasional glances from mums to each other as a child was being taken out back would say it all really, as the fathers tended to be firmer than the mothers.

I don't personally have a problem with smacking children in moderation, if not for the ludicrously unrealistic expectations placed upon them for such extended periods. This coupled with the embarrassment of being taken publically to the back room and back again (then walking more awkwardly from the pain) made the whole ordeal rather tortuous as a child.

If you disagree with me and are thinking this two-hour obligation seems perfectly reasonable, then try to consider the additional biannual assembly conventions, where the same demands were placed on children for (you've guessed it) up to three whole days. Not counting the two hours traveling time each way, we had to be good as gold from 9.30am through to 4pm, with only an hour's lunch-break (where only a slight lapse in behavioural perfection was permitted). As lucky as my schoolmates thought I was to have a Friday off in order to attend these conventions, little did they know that I would be spending three days doing absolutely nothing fun or exciting, not even remotely enjoyable. Having kissed goodbye to the weekend, it was straight back to school, without having enjoyed even a moment's respite.

As for school itself, being a Jehovah's Witness child was a real challenge. My primary school was a Church of England public school that had morning assembly for the entire two hundred and fifty pupils each and every day. At the end of each assembly we had a hymn to sing followed by a prayer, neither of which I was allowed to take part in. This was because they were not praying and singing to Jehovah God, just God (the unbranded one), so to be involved would be practicing interfaith, a sacrilege. Standing there with a closed mouth during the song, or open eyes during the prayer quickly made me a target of what were at first mere suspicious glances, soon to be followed by questions from my classmates and then the inevitable talking behind my back. This would in some instances escalate into ridicule and mocking. It was made worse when a teacher who was not aware of my beliefs (and therefore sincere reason for not participating in the activities) decided to get my attention in front of everyone and make me comply. The resulting embarrassment and subsequent persistent questioning from my peers made the whole thing rather unpleasant to say the least.

If there's one thing a child wants at school, it's to fit in and get along with his classmates. I quickly got used to the morning assembly routine, but there was always a special occasion on the horizon that I was to avoid getting involved with for the same reasons. If it wasn't Christmas, it was Easter, or Bonfire Night, Halloween, Valentine's Day, Remembrance Day, Mother's or Father's Day, or even the Harvest Festival, none of which Jehovah's Witnesses are allowed anything to do with. The real difficulty however came with birthday celebrations, since these were also forbidden. Having never celebrated my birthday, I had no knowledge of what I was missing. When someone said something like 'oh that must be horrible, not celebrating your birthday', I didn't really bat an eyelid. The beginnings of jealousy (albeit relatively mild) came when I would hear stories of what my peers were getting as gifts; all the wonderful toys, gadgets, games consoles etc. contributed to the feeling that I was missing out. I was however well trained as a Jehovah's Witness, so my feelings were quelled by the knowledge that I was pleasing God by having no part in these things.

Additional problems came when my well-meaning classmates would invite me to their birthday parties. Of course I could not go, and as a young child it wasn't easy trying to explain that whilst I was grateful for the invitation, I was unable to attend because I was a Jehovah's Witness and we don't celebrate birthdays. Of course the word soon spread and the mocking would ensue. Even the briefest of humiliating remarks cut deep and would make me cower whenever anything to do with my beliefs would come up in discussion.

I had one best friend at primary school, his name was Henry and he lived just up the road from me in a very large house with an equally large garden. His family was quite wealthy but they were genuinely kind and caring people and I very much enjoyed playing with Henry at their house (which I was permitted to do as they understood and respected our beliefs). It came as a great upset when in the third year of primary school, Henry was moved to a 'Middle School' and I never saw him again. It has only recently become clear that my parents permitted our friendship but did not encourage it. Only on a handful of occasions was I allowed to associate with any of my non-witness schoolmates.

I have fond memories of growing up in that little cottage, learning to ride my bike, playing in the makeshift summer house that Dad built for myself and my sister, and my much loved pet cat, Sam. We certainly had a sheltered upbringing and what we were allowed to watch on television was heavily restricted. We were not permitted to watch programmes like Power Rangers because there was fighting involved. We weren't allowed to watch Pokémon because the creatures 'evolved'. As we got older, we liked watching The Simpsons, which thankfully was tolerated by our parents, however if the word 'crap' was used more than once, that was it, off it went. Where possible, everything revolved around service to Jehovah, or at least that was the ideal we were aiming for. As a young child, the religious meetings were certainly boring as I've already described, but the encouragement was always there to find an answer or comment so we could participate. The many smiles and compliments afterwards that gave praise to us little ones were a great encouragement, and the desire to please was always strong. This was especially easy when the material on rare occasion happened to be aimed at children, or as was often the case, a question would be asked about one of the pictures in The Watchtower. At the end of every Sunday meeting there would be an arrangement for Field Service. Fortunately my family rarely stayed for this, my Dad instead preferring the Saturday morning arrangement. This decision received no complaints from any of us.

The door-to-door preaching work was always difficult for me. I firmly believed that I was doing God's will by calling on people and talking to them about the Bible and trying to get them to take copies of *The*

Watchtower and *Awake!* magazines, but I couldn't seem to understand why there was so much apathy and sometimes hatred from the people we called on. The explanation given for this was usually one of two. Firstly, Jesus was hated and persecuted for his teachings and he said that those who follow him would likewise suffer. Furthermore, because Satan is at present the ruler of the world, he is trying to stop God's true message from being spread. The second reason was usually to do with the fact that we live in a relatively wealthy country, where people have most things (if not everything) they need in life. They like their lifestyle of (apparent) greed and indulgence and therefore neither want, nor care for our message. Often, a brother or sister would mention that in particular countries, those who live in poverty are desperate to hear our message. They would say things like, "The truth is thriving out there..." which would make us all feel a bit better about ourselves.

A major reason for my not enjoying the preaching work (also called 'Ministry' or 'Field Service') was my fear of either calling on, or being seen by my school peers. For the few that could almost be called friends it was no problem, but anyone else would be a nightmare. Because our congregation's assigned territory (like most others) was also where I lived, there was a good chance I would see or be seen by someone I'd rather not. Here I was dressed up all smart and talking about God with a Bible in my hand. The comments, chants, and later bullying that would follow were a cause of much distress.

This became even more of an issue when I moved up to secondary school. It was 1997, and I'd reached the age of ten and therefore legally my sister and I could no longer share a bedroom. Also, mother was pregnant with her third child who turned out to be my little brother. After a fairly brief search, we settled on a three bedroom semi-detached house only half a mile from our little cottage. These were exciting times with all the changes going on, and I was fast growing up. Our new neighbours were pleasant on one side and ... interesting on the other. The three middle-aged brothers who lived on the pleasant side were really decent people. One of them in particular was always doing things to help our family. He would (and still does to this day) put out the bins, mow the lawn, trim the hedges and feed the cats if we ever went away, all for no charge. He'd accept a cup of tea or maybe a cold beer when he was mowing the lawn, but nothing more. The other two brothers were polite and friendly, though we didn't see them often for anything more than a passing greeting.

Our neighbours on the other side were also polite and friendly, though they appeared to never wash and their house had become a cave of hoarded items, newspapers, dirt, and more. On one occasion I came home from school and didn't have my key with me so they invited me in to wait until Mum came home. I sat delicately perched on a chair in their living room, trying to do some homework. It was a real challenge because the house literally stunk of a cocktail of indescribable foulness. Fearing the worst, I politely refused all offers of food or drink and waited for that glorious time when I could taste clean air. Once the time to leave finally arrived, I thanked them and made my way to the door. I had to squeeze through the hallway that was half blocked by a wall (which was taller than me) of old newspapers. As I reached the bottom of the stairs I caught a glimpse into their downstairs bathroom. The notion that these people, though kind, chose not to utilise the availability of water for self-cleaning was confirmed by the mountain of old clothes that filled their bathtub. I left through the jungle, or front garden if you will, and vowed never again to step a foot therein. That house and family would later be the start of a series of tragic events that changed both our families' lives forever.

Shortly after the wonderful arrival of my little brother, the giant Alsatian from two doors up the road killed my beloved pet and childhood friend, Sam the cat. I missed him dearly. It was my first real feeling of loss. There had previously been death in the family but I was too young to really understand. My Granddad on my Mum's side had died years ago and I'd never met him; my grandma was still alive. My Granddad on my Dad's side had committed suicide by hanging himself when I was very young so I barely remembered him, and grandma on that side had died just a few years later. I can just about recall images of her (Dad's side of the family were Witnesses while my mother was the only one from her family). All I can really remember from losing Sam the cat was the sadness because he was gone, and the fact that he wasn't going to be resurrected to the paradise as animals aren't included in God's promise, so I really was never going to see him again.

With the distractions of my little brother's arrival (whom I adored), moving house, and all the excitement and challenges from moving to secondary school, I inevitably moved on and we soon got another cat. On reflection, it doesn't seem fair that as part of God's original plan, animals were from the very start born into inevitable death. I doubt many Witnesses have considered that, or questioned why that might be the case. I digress…

Secondary school was a big change. There was more work to do, harder work, and now homework. I was a good lad, quite smart, but not a genius. I was certainly not one of the 'cool kids' though. My new school was also in the village but was naturally quite a bit larger than the one I had just left. There were about a thousand students attending at any one time so it was busier, louder, and at first a maze. I remember being issued with a map of the buildings, but all too often getting confused, with many of the corridors looking the same. I wanted to do well to please my parents and teachers so with enthusiasm I tackled everything my teachers threw at me. I was also very keen to share my beliefs with teachers and classmates. Knowing (and believing) I was pleasing God and could count the time for my monthly service report, I made conscious efforts to make the most of every opportunity to preach. I remember taking my own Bible to my religious education class, which didn't fuel any particular negative response from others, at least not that I was aware of. On another occasion I remember reading my Bible during morning registration and even handing out little Watchtower printed leaflets on various subjects.

This is where being a Witness was really tough. Anyone who was slightly different was instantly a target for mob ridicule. Some kids were nice enough, but every now and then someone would make a discourteous comment that would escalate into a barrage of humiliation that would follow me for the rest of the day. I remember arguing with my science teacher about evolution and the 'Big Bang' theory. Despite my opinion and Watchtower training, I really knew nothing about either, but I would still argue. By being outspoken both in and out of the classroom, I made myself a ready target for oppression. Things became even worse when I reached the second year. One particular 'tough guy' took a dislike to me because I was a Witness. Apparently he and his family hated them to a considerable degree. I never knew why exactly, but it didn't really matter at the time. I was too busy trying to avoid him without giving the appearance of fear. He'd like to show off to his mates by intimidating me verbally and physically in front of them. I didn't cower, but tried to stand my ground a little, without being aggressive in tone or body language. I was tiny compared to him, and I was on my own. There was no chance of me having any measure of success in a physical sense. Intellectual superiority didn't offer too much help either. The temptation for a hilarious rebuttal would achieve the desired effect in one sense, by making a fool of my schoolyard enemy. This moment of glorious triumph would be catastrophically brief and the retaliation would be far worse than had my mouth remained shut. My naivety shone through in this regard, but I quickly learned that in order to suffer minimally and retain my Christian approved conduct I had to settle for avoidance where possible and acceptance when not. The thought of reporting this abuse to teachers was suppressed by the fear of both nothing being done by them, and the potential worsening of the attacks.

On one cold, winters day, the school canteen was offering out hot soup in disposable cups with a piece of bread. Having enjoyed mine and disposed of the cup, I went outside for some fresh air. Upon turning a corner I became face to face with my nemesis and his band of moronic followers. Having said nothing to spark hostility, I was subjected to the usual pushing and shoving and mocking that I had become accustomed to. This was until Mr Tough Guy decided to pour his full cup of fresh and decidedly hot soup over my head. Upon fleeing the scene in both physical and emotional pain, I was granted assistance by two kind lads who'd seen what had happened. We went to our head-of-year teacher and reported the incident. As there were witnesses, action was taken. He had received a written warning and threat of suspension. This clearly angered him as outside of school he found me on a secluded woodland footpath on my way home and tried to strangle me, with hatred and anger so clear in his eyes. Luckily for me, someone I knew (an older student whose father was a Witness and happened to be physically huge and muscular) walked by, spotted what was happening, and intervened. Once freed, and with my attacker having fled, I carried on home, shaken, upset, and distraught. I have no shame in saying I cried when I got home, having experienced the escalation of abuse to a frightening level. My parents were supportive but didn't take the matter further. I suppose they left it to my judgement. This second incident, although having occurred outside of school, was handled well by the staff. My foe was expelled and I no longer had to contend with that particular persistent pest that was so abrasive to my wellbeing.

As I crossed the halfway point in my journey through secondary school, I had earned a little respect from many of my peers. I'd toughened up a bit and lessened my outspokenness as a Jehovah's Witness, which had certainly made me a smaller target. This lasted for a little while, until another troublesome individual decided to make me his periodic amusement. He was the same age, but clearly not of the same demeanour as myself, and had taken a liking to playing games of intimidation. He'd like to block my path repeatedly, trying to get me to snap and make physical contact where he could retaliate. He'd also flick my forehead with his finger with the same goal in mind. He was more careful than my previous opponent in that he'd be careful not to be seen. Rather than showing off to others, he would simply enjoy it for himself. This actually backfired, as on one occasion we had a scuffle outside in an overgrown part of the school playground. Nothing much came of the altercation in physical terms, but one of my school friends was nearby and saw what took place. He then proceeded to tell several people that I had beaten up this 'bully', when in reality a brief wrestle was all that took place with no clear winner or loser. Although I had said nothing, word soon spread and everyone believed it, despite the denial by the 'cool, tough guy'. My status was elevated for a time and he suffered immeasurably, which on reflection might have sparked a revenge attack. The final result though was rather pleasing; he left me alone. I grew a little more that day.

Having gained a little respect and confidence, I was able to subtly make it known that I wasn't prepared to 'take any crap'. I certainly wasn't one of the tough guys all of a sudden, but I was no longer the easy and obvious target I had once been. I had made a couple more friends (despite it being strongly discouraged by my religion), and this made school life far easier. I was able to have fun, make jokes, laugh and be laughed with, which was great. There were three of us, smart, funny, and good for each other. We had the same interests - computers, video games, and motor racing. They knew about my beliefs and were respectful, but I'd decided to keep below the radar and keep these to myself to get by. I soon learned that letting myself swear from time to time would gain me more acceptance in general. In effect I had started to lead a 'double life' as *The Watchtower* had so regularly and vigorously warned about. At the meetings I was a sweet humble servant of God, at school I was nearly a normal young man, like the rest.

Keeping the beliefs to myself didn't always work, as from time to time someone would ask me, "Are you a Jehovah?" or something similar in front of a group of people. I'd reluctantly acknowledge that yes, indeed I was. I would here mutterings of jokes being told behind my back with terms like 'Bible-Basher', 'Joho', and even 'Jehovah's Biscuit' (which I never understood). This however was not the worst of it, as one time, in my last year, a teacher had arranged a presentation with a few students sitting in front of everyone. I was asked to participate, which I did, and took my place on a comfortable sofa and was given a cup of tea and biscuit. As I pondered the nature of this peculiar event that I was a part of, the teacher was explaining that very important life-saving work was going on. All you do is sit down and have a free cup of tea and a biscuit, while you GIVE BLOOD. At that moment she slapped a large sticker on my chest that said 'Give Blood'. I felt terrible as I sat there endorsing donation of blood for transfusions, something my religion regarded as disgusting to God. I couldn't wait to get away and take off the ghastly sticker. I felt like a traitor and was dreading the comments that would mock my momentary hypocrisy. The comments never came though, which was a relief, but my conscience was affected. It took me a while to forgive myself, although there was no real blame on my part. As a Witness though I was always scrutinising my actions to see if I'd slipped up anywhere, which is where the problem lays. My guilty conscience was telling me that I should have got up and left the moment I realised what the presentation was about. Out of fear of embarrassment I stayed, keeping quiet, and keen not to draw any attention to myself. This type of conflict had plagued me to a varying degree for my whole school life.

My exams had come and gone and I was freed from the grasp of compulsory education. I had to decide what to do with my life at this point. Despite the discouragement from the Watchtower publications, I decided to attend Sixth Form. This was at the same school, and so was a familiar place with familiar people. I studied Information Technology (I.T.), Business, and Health & Social Care. Had I been given the choice, I wouldn't have picked the last one, but they make you choose three. I.T. was my interest; I was fascinated by technology, particularly computers. Unfortunately, the I.T. course was all about spreadsheets, databases, and word processing. My interest was in the inner workings - I wanted to learn what all the components did, take them apart and put them back together again. None of this was being taught in these classes so I was left feeling both disappointed and bored. I had made a decent effort of my first year but decided to abandon this avenue of education after the exams and look for work.

Unlike many a young person who didn't really know what kind of career or job would be the one for them, I knew exactly what I wanted and was determined to get it. My enthusiasm and desire to devour as much knowledge on the subject made me an appealing prospect to the local computer company. The nice family had not intended to employ anyone but being so impressed, offered me a job. I loved it, and learnt quickly becoming a useful asset to the business. I had a day off in the week so chose to expand my door-to-door preaching work. I was keen at this point to make a fresh start and get my faith back on track. Everything was looking up for me and I had no troublesome foes to deal with. I had money coming in and an exciting new life to enjoy.

My place of work was only about a mile away from our house, which meant I could cycle easily back and forth. I remember at this point I pondered where life would take me, what it had in store, and what I could potentially achieve. My next goal was to learn to drive. After saving as much money as possible and reaching the point when I felt I was ready to give it a shot, I enquired around the congregation about a recommendation for a suitable driving instructor. A couple of people suggested a chap in the same town as the Kingdom Hall (Church), so I gave him a call.

I'd awaited the arrival of our agreed first lesson with nervous anticipation. As it happens, he was a fine teacher and all round pleasant and friendly person. Knowing he'd taught Witnesses before it was a goal of mine to share some snippets of my beliefs where possible, counting the time of course. Upon reaching a suitable opportunity, I'd started describing various aspects of the religion. He was respectfully curious and we had enjoyable conversations, but it went no further. I remember calling on his house a few times whilst on the door-to-door work, and had on a couple of occasions offered him *The Watchtower* and *Awake!* magazines. He always respectfully declined, which was disappointing at the time, but now I realise his head was most certainly screwed on.

It was around this time I had made the choice to get baptised, and cement my position as one of Jehovah's Witnesses. I felt the time must be right as I was approaching nineteen years of age. From experience I was aware of frequent talk amongst members of the congregation about someone approaching the age of twenty who was yet to be baptised. People would often speculate that the person was lacking in faith, immature, or perhaps feeling guilty over some undisclosed wrongdoing. This, among other subtly instilled pressures had only one effect on me - I had to get baptised. It is almost considered a sin to be an adult who knows 'the truth' and yet for some reason holds back from getting baptised. After all, Jehovah is holding out his hand in personal invitation to you. Would you make him wait? These are the kind of attitudes that work themselves into the discussions at meetings and the pages of *The Watchtower*.

When I told me parents that I wanted to get baptised they were thrilled. Not only would I be making them proud, and pleasing Jehovah God, I would be setting a good example for my younger sister and brother. In order to take this step I had to undertake a meeting with three Elders, each on a separate occasion. We would discuss questions from the book 'Organized to Accomplish Our Ministry', which has since been revamped and renamed as 'Organized to do Jehovah's Will'. The book had eighty questions, designed to test the knowledge of the individual. A few examples are:

"Who is the true God?"

"What attitude should Christians show toward those who serve as shepherds in the congregation?"

"In God's arrangement, who is head of a married woman?"

"What is God's law concerning blood?"

"Against what spiritistic practices employed by the Devil and his demons does the Bible warn us?"

> "By what means will God destroy the wicked?"
>
> "What urgent work does the Bible set out for all Christians at this time?"

If the questions as a whole are answered satisfactorily, and the individual is not known to be committing any wrongdoing that may require adjustment, the Elders will allow him to be baptised at the next circuit or district assembly. As I was granted with an affirmative answer to my request, I readied myself for the next assembly, due in November. Fortunately it was a circuit assembly, as that was my preference, mostly because it was indoors and therefore a much warmer climate than district assemblies held at football stadiums. They day finally came and my whole family was excited for me. I would be getting up with others in front of about a thousand people, where we would in turn be dipped under the water as a public declaration of our dedication to Jehovah God. The actual baptism is preceded by a special baptismal talk that praises those who have chosen this path. It usually features encouragement to set 'spiritual goals' such as expanding your preaching work by pioneering, or serving at Bethel. Often there is also a warning of the probability that trouble may follow this decision to get baptised, as the Devil hates God and those who serve him. Having heard the talk, the speaker then invited all the baptismal candidates to stand. There are two final questions that are then asked:

> "On the basis of the sacrifice of Jesus Christ, have you repented of your sins and dedicated yourself to Jehovah to do his will?"
>
> "Do you understand that your dedication and baptism identify you as one of Jehovah's Witnesses in association with God's spirit-directed organization?"

After responding aloud with a 'yes' to both questions, we were declared as qualified and directed to the backstage changing area. Once ready in our modest swimwear, we formed an orderly queue to the pool, where we waited in turn, to be baptised. Each submersion and subsequent emergence was greeted with a round of applause from the audience. My turn came and I did not hesitate. I entered the warm yet small pool and after a few moments, was dipped under the water. My exit from the water prompted the applause that I had seen so often before given to other people. As I walked up the steps and out of the pool, I was handed my towel and directed back to the changing rooms. Upon my return to the auditorium friends and family congratulated me. Hugs, cards and gifts followed; it was a special time. Now I was baptised, I could be used more for congregational responsibilities. I asked to be on the 'sound team' at the Kingdom Hall. This meant that during meetings I would help with the microphones, arranging the seating on the platform, and operate the main sound console. It wasn't too much later that I was asked occasionally to stand before the congregation and offer an opening or closing prayer. My progress in this regard brought me respect from other members of the congregation, and to some extent a sense of higher worth.

CHAPTER 3

LIFE AS A WITNESS

ADULTHOOD

It was about a year later that I required a relatively minor but invasive surgical procedure, the location of which was should we say, sensitive. I was, to put it mildly, terrified of the impending visit to the hospital theatre. This dread instinctively caused me to pray, and this brought me closer to Jehovah (my personal relationship with God could be summed up by such drawing to and from, depending on my level of need or worry at any particular time). The first consultant visit was all very reassuring and went well, with a nice friendly English doctor. My second visit however was less so. Hospitals, to me at least, are unpleasant at the best of times and the consulting doctor was of Asian descent. Although I was not a racist, I felt uncomfortable, not least because his English was distinctly questionable. I had to at some point during this visit broach the subject of blood transfusions. Although my mother was with me for support, we had agreed it would look best if I mentioned it. Neither of us wanted to give the impression that the decision was being made for me. On reflection though, I felt I had no choice. My mother had not put this pressure on me at all, at least not directly in this instance. It had come from the belief system that was firmly indoctrinated within both my conscious and subconscious mind. The decision was a 'no brainer'; there was no possibility that I would consent to accepting blood, under any circumstances. The very thought of taking blood was disgusting to me. My thinking was rooted in agreement with *The Watchtower's* description of all the diseases and complications that transfused blood is (apparently) riddled with, and how abhorrent the procedure is to God.

Having not expressed this disgust to the consultant, but instead simply making clear that I was outright refusing a transfusion, I handed him a copy of my Advanced Medical Directive. This form was a Watchtower designed legal document that outlined what the hospital could and couldn't legally do to my body regarding blood. There were a couple of areas where, as an individual, I had to choose regarding blood fractions. These were not specifically mentioned in the Bible, and therefore were classified as a 'conscience matter'. The bottom of the form contained my signature along with those of two witnesses, who of course were also Jehovah's Witnesses. The Elders held a copy of the form in the safe at the Kingdom Hall. Should any legal dispute arise, they could assist (along with the Watchtower's Hospital Liaison Committee which exists solely for this purpose) and make sure that I would die rather than accept blood.

The consultant doctor was seemingly fine with this proviso and wrote the following on my surgery consent form:

> 'PATIENT IS AGAINST BLOOD TRANSFUSIONS IF IT IS NECCESSARY (JEHOVAH WITNESS)"

I remember that after leaving the hospital with my copy of the agreement, I was a little worried about the wording of this statement. I wasn't convinced it was clear enough. I didn't have the confidence to go back in and make them change it, plus I had submitted the medical directive. I therefore trusted in God to make sure his will would be done.

I had to wait about six months for the operation, which was a period of dreaded anxiety. I was embarrassed about the nature of the surgery and knew that my employers (though lovely) would probe a little further than I wanted them to had I divulged the true but personal reality. Instead I told them it was an operation on my foot, which I had in fact already previously received. Yes I lied, or if not at least I had told a half-truth. Neither of which was acceptable to a Witness, but I imagine many others had done the same kind of thing from time to time, claiming it to be a moment of weakness.

The time finally came and Mum took me to the hospital for the procedure. I wasn't allowed to eat at all before the operation. The letters NBM were written on the whiteboard above my bed. I figured this meant 'No Blood Medicine' but this was later corrected to 'Nil By Mouth' (the no food thing). Nevertheless it wasn't long before I was handed a dressing gown, which was to be my single item of attire. Only a quarter of an hour passed before a pair of nurses came to take me into theatre. I lay helpless in my bed whilst they wheeled me down the corridor and into the unknown. I was brought into the anaesthetist's chamber where I was greeted by welcoming and friendly faces and felt almost like royalty. Having been put mildly at ease I experienced the cold feeling in my left arm as the knockout mixture entered my body. Mere seconds later my vision went briefly fuzzy and I drifted off. It was the best sleep imaginable, although I don't recall dreaming.

I awoke in stages, first coming round very disorientated and fumbling around with my hand at the sore area below, although not aware I was doing so. The nurse assigned to observe my return to consciousness had to keep moving my hand away from my wound, so as to stop me from messing up their handiwork. I had no knowledge of how long I was unconscious for, but it can't have been more than a couple of hours. After the observation period I was moved back to the ward where the small bag containing my belongings was. In the bedside cabinet I had stored my Bible and a couple of Watchtower published books, although I never picked them up to read. I was more interested in what was for lunch and the novelty of my own television and phone. I decided on the snooker to distract me from the pain. After a few hours of lying there I became determined to go home rather than stay the night. The surgeons wanted me to remain for at least one night to check for swelling. The Matron however sided with me and at around eight o'clock she said I could go home. I was given some strong painkillers and discharged. I had about a week off work and then was back to fighting form, feeling this unpleasant chapter was now behind me.

A few months later I passed my driving test and bought a car. My little red run-around was my own ticket to freedom. I could go anywhere I wanted to without having to ask for a lift. I used my car to get involved more in the door-to-door preaching work and to take older Witnesses to the Kingdom Hall for the meetings. My personality was developing nicely and I was flourishing as an individual. Pretty much everything was going well for me at this point.

This began to change when I began to suffer from post-operative pain, though I didn't believe it could be that at the time. I was stricken with a nasty, dull pulsating pain that radiated up and down the inside of my legs and through my groin. Though not cripplingly severe, it was quite unpleasant. Imagine you've been kicked in the genitalia; after the worst of the pain departs you're still left with a throbbing ache that won't leave you for a while. Now imagine this coming and going all of the time, and you're pretty much there. I found it particularly distressing, as it would be there every day without fail. My doctors had informed me that it was referred pain caused by my surgery and was surprisingly common, which helped, but only a little. I was daunted by the prospect of this becoming a lifelong feature. A little while after this I also began feeling physically unwell all of the time. I was nearly always nauseous, which became especially worse after eating. I was constantly exhausted and suffered with regular stomach trouble. This persisted for months on end and as a result, I became rather depressed. Not wanting to let on too much that I was suffering to this extent, (apparently a male trait) I tried to hide it where possible.

This feeling of being constantly ill had all but overshadowed the pain, which itself acted as the icing on the cake. Thus they collectively kept me utterly miserable. I had all but chosen to suffer alone, which can't have helped my situation. I was talking to God all the time, constantly praying, sharing my frustrations and sadness for feeling so consistently below par. I felt there was no solution in sight. After a while however it somehow became just a little more manageable and I regained some control, though I would continue to face bouts of relapse from time to time.

It was soon after this period that a family of Witnesses that had known me for my whole life offered me a job. They ran a carpentry business and I was feeling like perhaps a change in employment would be beneficial. My technical skills were rather useful and I helped the business to expand rapidly by taking the company online. I was still suffering on and off with this bothersome affliction, but had things under control for a little while at least. After a few months however, it returned to the forefront of my mind and was affecting me exactly how it had done before. I worked hard every day at work, but even holding a smile had become near impossible. I would go home exhausted and pretty much go straight to bed. Sleeping all evening and night I would awake and repeat the same process the next day. The fight to make it through each and every day took all the strength I had within me. I didn't know why I was this way, or what I could do to combat it. I don't know how my dad felt about me at this point. I sometimes remember the disappointment that he showed when I would not want to come out on the door-to-door preaching work, or when I didn't want to go to the meeting. Mum showed more sympathy, but I don't think she understood what was going through my head, probably because I didn't talk much. I was very depressed, and had even by this point considered the possibility of suicide. I just couldn't face life anymore. Every waking moment was almost unbearable and my thoughts were all over the place. I was praying to God for an answer and some relief, but none came. I didn't give up on Jehovah though, as I was so desperate for the promised paradise to come and take away all my problems.

One thing that struck me was how I had never imagined what it was like to feel this way, but also to not understand why. I had been to the doctor numerous times and had countless tests done which all came back normal. The doctor was telling me I was either stressed or depressed, but probably both. I tried the prescribed medication for depression, which helped for a while and I was able to make some progress.

It was around this period that my sister had made good progress in 'the truth' and was looking to get baptised. She had the required three meetings (or interviews if you will), each with a different Elder. They concluded that she could get baptised at the next Circuit or District Convention. Then without warning she announced that she wasn't ready and couldn't go through with it. We were all shocked. She did not give me a reason, nor did I ask. Mum explained that she was upset by something that was said during her final interview, though no more details were uncovered until much later. This rejection hurt the whole family to some degree. Those who know 'the truth' and do not act in accordance with God's commands will certainly perish at his hand during Armageddon. There is also a degree of shame that a family feels when a child turns their back on God.

Around a year later she found herself a boyfriend who was not a Witness. This was a big deal for my parents, though overall I think they handled it well. He was a local lad who seemed nice, but of course was part of 'the world', and therefore not to be trusted. My parents chose to have him in for a 'chat' and laid out their viewpoint, which was of course that they didn't condone the relationship but could not stop it. They also made an effort to explain our beliefs as Witnesses. The ultimate goal, which was destined to remain a fantasy, was that he would come into 'the truth' with my sister at some point in the future. I was too distracted by my own struggle to delve too deeply into her affairs. I respected her choice to do with her life what she pleased. At this time she announced that she didn't want to have anything to do with the religion anymore. Our parents took this very hard and resorted to heavy pressure to the point of bullying her until she went to a meeting. After a while though, they realised this course of action was futile and settled on repeated nagging in hope of bringing her back to the faith.

Once I had managed to get myself back to regular Witness meetings, I was soon recognised for my comments that were filled with feeling and warm praise for God and the hope we all shared. The talks that I gave from the platform were also awash with powerful and emotional sentiments about God's imminent new system, that I sometimes evoked tears from members of the congregation. I had developed such an emotional attachment to Jehovah God that on outward appearance I was 'spiritually strong' and faithful. On the inside I was barely held together, suffering to the point of tears, but unable to share the thoughts that troubled me so much. Thoughts that even I couldn't understand. The following few years were to be a struggle indeed, especially with the developments that would soon take place...

One Sunday morning (February, 2008) I had woken early to the sound of muffled shouting next door. The room that I shared with my brother was right next to the one belonging to the forty-five year old daughter of next door's family. She was shouting, and I remember hearing sounds of things falling down and crashing to the floor. She was crying out 'Help! I can't breathe'. I was only just beginning to fully wake up and was starting to make sense of what she was saying when I heard a very loud bang on the door. Our whole family got up and we all moved quickly downstairs and out of the house. Upon exiting the front door we saw the father and middle-aged son next door exiting their house. Smoke was bellowing out of their mouths as they coughed and choked, desperate for oxygen. Their house was on fire and had been for some time. We stood in shock, seeing the blaze that had engulfed the house attached to our own. A group of neighbours had already gathered outside. There was shouting from the upstairs front bedroom window. The mother was still up there, screaming for help. She had the window open and was gasping for air. Everyone was taking a moment to work out what to do; the fire was too intense to go into the house. The mother started to scream 'my back is burning'! It was at this moment my dad appeared from the back of our house with a ladder. He threw it against the wall, and ran up it. I jumped on the bottom to give it some stability. He had to convince the 70-odd year old to climb out of the window. She was terrified. How he lifted a sixteen stone woman out of that window and carried her down that ladder I simply do not know. He was a strong man, but not a body builder. Later on I found out that he had in fact hurt his back rather badly.

Once she was out of immediate danger I noticed that their son (in his thirties) was shivering and in shock. I gave him my winter coat that I had grabbed on the way out and asked someone to watch him. We had heard nothing from their daughter since leaving the house. The mother was crying out for her, which was upsetting to hear. My dad, two neighbours, and myself rushed round the back to see if there was hope of getting into her bedroom with the ladder. The house was an inferno at this point with flames bursting out of the living room window, preventing access to her room.

A minute or two later the fire brigade arrived; four fire engines in total. Smoke was now leaking out of our roof tiles, so they went into our house and soaked the attic with water to prevent the fire from spreading. No doubt the stacks of newspapers and associated clutter had fuelled the fire into a furnace, as it was now raging. It took over four hours to put out the blaze. Unfortunately the daughter next door had died. We don't know exactly how the fire started, or why the father and son didn't get the rest of the family out of the house before trying to fight it. Equally, they didn't care to warn us about the dangerous situation that we were unknowingly in. I am eternally grateful to the neighbour from down the road who raised the alarm and called the emergency services. Once the fire was eventually extinguished, the coroner arrived to retrieve the body of our sadly deceased neighbour.

Shortly after midday, a few of the brothers from the congregation arrived including our Book Study Overseer. They were kind, helpful and supportive. We had briefly spoken to the local council representative, who had promised us emergency accommodation, but couldn't guarantee where it would be. My dad was worried about leaving the house unattended, especially as he had all of his work tools stored in the adjacent sheds. Our Book Study Overseer kindly offered for us to stay at his house until we sorted ourselves out. My brother and I stayed in the living room and our parents had the spare room upstairs. My sister stayed with another family to spread the burden slightly. We were there for only a week, as the primary school was very generous and gave us use of their three-bedroom caretaker's house that was presently unoccupied. As it was only half a mile from our temporarily abandoned home it was very convenient. It was also a little comforting to not be displaced to an unfamiliar town.

I can't fault the congregation here; they were very helpful with the move. Several families had turned up to load their vehicles and transport our undamaged belongings to our new abode. With this support, the task had become decidedly easier and less arduous than it would have been without. We rather quickly grew fond of our new home, which was substantially larger and very comfortable. We didn't know where our neighbours had been moved to until quite a bit later. To be honest, we were rather angry with them and their foolishness that had caused all this trouble. The worst however, was still to come.

It was around this time in my life that I began to question the beliefs I had been raised with. I would no longer accept everything I was told, but rather would ask why it was so. I wouldn't accept the answer given either, unless I was fully satisfied. During our family study time this would infuriate Dad, which led to a noticeable divide developing between us. I was finally standing up to him rather than just cowering into submission as I had been raised to do. I was not rebelling against authority, rather just challenging the authority to prove itself. The authority being the Watchtower Society rather than Dad, though I doubt he saw it this way. I wouldn't let myself just blindly accept everything as I had done my whole life. My personal suffering had bred a new me, more cynical with a sceptical outlook and certainly a far cry from the Jehovah's Witness ideal. The Watchtower describes this as 'independent thinking' or an 'independent spirit':

> "We need to guard against developing a spirit of independence. By word or action, may we never challenge the channel of communication that Jehovah is using today." - *The Watchtower*, Nov 15th 2009.

The above example is one of many statements printed in Watchtower Society literature that triggers feelings of guilt in Witnesses who dare to have doubts about their religious leadership. It is highly unlikely that an active Witness will realise this though, I certainly didn't. While my attitude probably came as a shock to my parents, it's quite interesting to note that after the initial upset had settled, Dad actually seemed to respect me a little more. It was either that or he was afraid of pushing me further in the direction of critical thinking or resentment. I'm not sure which of these was true, but to some degree it could have been both.

The school head teacher wasn't charging us a penny in rent for the home he so graciously lent us. This kindness prompted my dad to offer to do some skilled jobs on the school grounds, one of which I helped him with. We erected a fence together at the rear entrance. This was one of the few times where we worked together and bonded, albeit only a little. It was a surreal feeling, having a 'father and son moment', especially as they were so rare. I didn't really understand my conflicting feelings towards him. I knew he was a good man in general, always willing to help people in the congregation. He just was rather tyrannical as a father, prone to anger outbursts, and either reluctant or unable to show love, at least not to his children. He'd been better with my younger brother but he probably wouldn't ever have won any parenting awards.

Not too long after we undertook this task together, Dad started to get a strange pain under his groin. This bore a quite bizarre similarity to my own affliction, but we only were able to discuss it briefly due to our unease with each other. He was also suffering with a low platelet count, meaning his blood wouldn't clot if he cut himself. I remember taking him to the hospital a couple of times to undergo tests to determine the cause. He was started on a treatment of steroids to boost his production of platelets. The side effects of this medication completely changed his personality. He became softer, more sensitive, and a borderline wimp. He started hugging us, and helping us with things we needed doing, and taking an interest in us so much more.

We didn't react with open arms; rather we were suspicious and standoffish, trying to make sense of the total change of character. I know I felt I couldn't just drop the years of hurt and misery he had caused with his anger and strict discipline. His behaviour would not be believed by members of the congregation, who saw him as a loyal, caring follower of Jehovah. Even Mum had to admit how she had been deeply saddened by his treatment of us over the years, and knew it was far from the loving care that 'True Christians' should be aspiring to. It was barely a few weeks of this behaviour before the unimaginable happened.

It was one sunny afternoon in May around three o'clock, when my boss came in to the office and asked me to go outside to see his son (the other boss). I complied and was met with a hug by the son. He said that something has happened to my dad and they were to take me home straight away. I was strangely calm, thinking he may have taken a turn for the worse with his platelets or something. My mind had also drifted to thoughts that he had even taken a knife to his wrists and was in the bath, dead or nearly so. They didn't tell me anything else and I didn't ask. The fifteen-minute drive home was almost silent, with little being said. I assumed it could not possibly be the worst scenario, but it was.

Upon arriving at the schoolhouse, I saw a police car and one officer standing outside. There was another inside who directed me to the living room. Mum was there, with my younger brother and sister and a couple of Witnesses. She had the unpleasant task of telling me that my dad had in fact died that morning. I took in this information, but didn't really react. I was more concerned with how everyone else was feeling rather than myself. I was in denial at this point, unable to believe he was gone. There were tears from Mum and both my siblings (as well as our guests) but not from me. Not until I saw his body later on. The years of working as a landscaper had meant he was an expert at tying knots, having had to secure his lawn mowers and other tools to his truck. His skill in this area had enabled him to expertly take his own life in the woods not far from our temporary accommodation. His decision to hang himself mirrored that of his father's, which now seemingly a family trait is one I insist on defying.

There was a perfectly understandable unease in the room as our guests were trying to be there for us but not knowing what to say after the initial hugs and sympathies. There were moments of silence, practical talk, and even some humour. All of which served as methods of coping for each of us in our own way. Over the course of the afternoon, various Witnesses arrived to offer support and condolence. As new visitors arrived, others left, so as not to overcrowd us. The support at this time of need could really not be faulted. There was much love, compassion, and further offerings to do chores or anything else that we needed.

Mum hadn't told my brother much about what had happened. I felt he ought to have more information so I took him outside and gave him a basic overview, without too much detail. I told him that Dad had gone to the woods and strangled himself. I can't decide if this was the right thing to do or not. Was I too vague, or not accurate enough? I simply don't know, but I had to tell him something other than just that his dad had died. I know that I would have needed to know more. He was tearful as I explained to him, but I think he was grateful to have gained just a little understanding, if nothing else.

After a few hours the police officers informed us that we could, if we wished go and see Dad's body. For myself, it was not even a question. I had to see him. I couldn't live the rest of my life taking someone else's word that he had died. The police officer made arrangements to take Mum and myself to the Chapel of Rest where the body had been prepared for viewing. We were taken through to a room with low light where his body was. He was lying motionless on a bed. His skin was a shade of pale grey I could never have pictured, and he was ice cold to touch. His stubble was as rough as sandpaper. We all shed tears whilst a prayer was said, asking Jehovah to watch over us and to request that Dad was resurrected in the New System. Upon concluding our visit I decided to kiss my dad on the forehead. I have only just come to realise that this was me forgiving him for everything he had done wrong, including taking his own life. I would harbour no resentment or disgust towards him. He had done the best he could to raise us despite his own suffering along the way. Was he perfect? Not a chance! But he was after all, my dad. Out of the mire of criticism, disappointment, and bouts of anger that had shaped me, lies a young man with a kind moral heart, a reasonable intellect, and glimmers of great potential.

The next day was truly bizarre. I can't remember how I slept, but remember clearly waking with the confusion that probably faces everyone who loses someone suddenly. There's a minute or two while your brain frantically tries to work out if the person is really gone. Was it just a dream? When you realise that it wasn't a dream you are struck with a pain in the pit of your stomach. The sadness and shock that immediately follows comes as a terrible repeat performance of the day before. Only at that moment there is no one to comfort you, and this time it is somehow more real. I remember feeling confused and vulnerable, naturally turning to Jehovah for support, just talking to him as you would a best friend. As the rest of the family gradually woke we said little to each other. Our family was missing its tyrant and it's provider. We had lost our strict leadership in one night and gained something we had dreamed of; freedom. I felt such a mixture of emotions including sadness, confusion, relief, and guilt. The guilt came from the relief, as I felt like such a bad person for experiencing it. He was my dad though, and he did love us, even if he barely knew how to show it.

The weather on this day was the same as the day before, unusually hot and sunny. I remember that around eleven in the morning visitors started to show up. More Witnesses had come to offer support and make sure we were coping. I couldn't explain how I felt to anyone, as I did not know myself. I liked the attention and loving care that was offered, which was something I had not really felt for as long as I could remember. People were really there for Mum and my siblings, but I don't think people knew how to approach me. I was more distant and kept my emotions to myself. This may have made it more difficult for people to really give me the comfort I needed. Some of the older Sisters in the congregation really tried though which helped, but I would not open up. I had decided to focus purely on the practical, whilst ignoring the emotional. This, it would seem, was to my detriment, but is apparently not uncommon in men. Plenty of non-Witnesses also came to offer condolence and brought cakes and other food so we wouldn't go hungry. The school even said we could stay at the house as long as we needed to. Nothing was too much trouble.

On the third or forth day after Dad's passing, the Brother who had put us up for a week after the fire had come round to help me go through paperwork. This was important, as I had to make multiple phone calls to inform people that Dad had died. Sorting through his papers I discovered that Dad had also seen fit to provide for us by having multiple life insurance policies as well as a pension fund. Upon discovering the amount that we should expect to receive, I was greatly relieved. I had been deeply worried that I would need to start earning more than three times the amount I was currently in order to cover the family expenses. The lifting of this burden brought tears to my eyes.

Many Brothers and Sisters invited us round for meals during the first couple of weeks. This was very kind, as we needed much support to help us find our feet. We didn't make it to meetings in the first week, but were graced with a warm welcome when we started going back during the second. After a short while though, the help began to wane and the smothering of kindness had all but stopped. They were there for us in the time of crisis but it did not last, nor could it. This could be entirely natural, as we needed to stand up as a family, which we could not have done if permanently sheltered. People are spur of the moment at times and the novelty of a family in need naturally wears off. Not to mention that people need to get on with their own busy lives. I can't help feeling though that the support structure was broken just a little too quickly. That is my only criticism, if I am permitted to make one.

I was now the man of the house and had important responsibilities, including caring for the family's spiritual needs. I had to lead the family Bible study and say the family prayer before each meal. My prayers were far more meaningful than the routine and standardised efforts that Dad had lazily settled on. I also tried to make the family study interesting and even fun where possible, a far cry from what we were used to. After a while however, my enthusiasm had diminished somewhat, but I was still making an effort. My prayers in front of the congregation were even more deeply thought-out and filled with emotion. This brought me respect from the congregation and plenty of invitations for further offerings. My talks from the platform had also become even more powerful and emotive, particularly when I touched on death or the resurrection. They were moving and encouraging, which rewarded me with sympathy as well as respect. I wasn't playing on the feelings of others; rather I was using the opportunity to delve into the shut book that contained my untouched and even undiscovered emotions. I'd muddled through so far without opening up to anyone directly, and I wasn't in a rush to now either. However, I wanted people to know that there were deep feelings behind my dry and sometimes numb persona. In private I'd talk to God as often as I felt necessary which, depending on how low I felt would be either once a day or as often as four or five times. The truth of the matter was that I was now rather lost inside, not knowing really who I was or why I even existed. With no understanding of how I felt or what was reality and what was a dream, I began to crave sleep. While unconscious I was at a place where I had no troubles, and my mind could rest.

I had slowly slipped back to feeling ill all of the time and my head was a mess. Without relief I battled through each day, barely managing to hold myself together as I was so exhausted. I had long dreamt of finding a partner to explore the feelings that ran deep yet were never shared with anyone other than God, whom of course never replied. I had a dream of finding someone special, who would help me make sense of my life and show me how to enjoy it, leaving my troubles behind. I eventually became torn between my love of the idea of a kind and caring God who was waiting to rid the world of all it's sorrows and restore peace, and my disappointment and frustration with the delay in it's arrival. I began to feel despondent about the promises that had been made by the Watchtower Society. Where was this New System, this paradise world, where not a problem exists? How long does God really need to prove his point to Satan about who has the right to rule the universe? These questions had started to form inside my head, and were not quashed by the years of absorbed Watchtower information and reasoning. They began to fester, though unexpressed outside of my thoughts.

The one thing that had given me happiness and temporary relief (other than the support from my little brother) was my recently acquired friendship with Jake. He was a fellow Witness who had moved into our congregation with his family a few years back. His family were always nice to me, but I had never really got to know him. There was a good reason for this; he was too popular. I remember seeing him at the meetings with a swarm of kids around him, everyone wanted to be Jake's friend. I didn't harbour any jealousy or resentment, but just didn't get in with that crowd. At the time, I became pretty good friends with his stepbrother who shared my cynical humour. After the loss of Dad however, somehow Jake and I became friends. What started as mere knowledge of each other's existence went on to become a fused bond that would survive, in spite of whatever was thrown at us. Our interests were very similar and we grew to have a sense of humour that could seemingly rival some of the world's greatest comedic efforts. Such was our friendship that we would often finish each other's sentences and even the subtlest of references to anything covertly said would be picked up and acknowledged with a wink, nod or grin. Jake had (whether he knew it or not) helped me through one of the most difficult parts of my life. I was about to do the same for him.

We were both in our early twenties when shockingly Jake was diagnosed with prostate cancer. This is incredibly rare in someone so young, but here he was facing the ultimate in an unsure future. We didn't know what was going to happen to him, but all I could do was be there for him, as he had been for me. In typical male fashion, the art of getting through a crisis is humour, coupled with a suitably distracting activity. Humour we already had plenty of, the distraction was the next choice to make. Some people in our situation would throw themselves at their religion for solace. I'm sure Jake had considered or even tried that before, but it can't have helped, as the solace was found elsewhere. We settled on a particular video game to play together. We clocked up countless hours ridding the world of virtual terrorists (shamelessly rebelling against the Jehovah's Witness view of such violent games). Such was our devotion to the perfection of this game that we'd play it on the hardest difficulty whilst using only pistols to defeat our electronic enemies. On occasion, we would pull an 'all-nighter', with cans of energy drinks and snacks on hand to keep us both conscious and lucid. The morning after would typically be a Sunday, where we would face the meeting whilst combatting the effects of caffeine and sugar overdose along with the craving for sleep. On too many occasions had we forgotten that we were on microphone duty and therefore had to make earnest efforts to appear normal whilst enduring this self inflicted artificial hangover. I remember standing at the back of the hall, with *The Watchtower* magazine and microphone in hand, waiting whilst the paragraph was being read out (possibly one proclaiming the wickedness of violent video games). My body swaying back and forth, struggling to remain balanced. Jake too was feeling the same effects. It was as comical as it was sad really, but it shows where I think we both were at that point with regards to life and 'the truth'. I cannot accurately speak for Jake, nor would it be right to, so I'll stick with myself. I had grown weary of the endless requirements that the religion places on each individual. Feeling the way I had been, whilst fighting to fulfil my work obligations, as well as the mountain that was meetings, study, and ministry work, literally took every ounce of energy I had.

There was no let-up, no relief from the 'spiritual duties' (known to Witnesses as 'privileges'. Whatever you did, there was always a *Watchtower* article or talk at the Kingdom Hall encouraging you to do more. I always felt guilty that I was not doing everything I could, despite the reality being that I was already pushing myself beyond my limits. I was divided now, as part of me was exhausted, the real me whose beliefs and convictions were slipping. The other part was my spiritual side, the part that deep down still believed in Jehovah and was desperate for his love and promised cure-filled intervention. There was only so long that these two identities could co-exist, as the internal conflict was as torturous as it was indescribably tiring.

In the mean time Jake had some *good* news, the diagnosis was wrong, he didn't have cancer after all. The downside however was that the medication the doctors had rushed to give him had all but destroyed his bladder. Poor chap; he still suffers to this day with excruciating pain among other things. I think one thing is clear – we would not have been able to cope with everything we went through had we not had each other. Here was a friendship where either of us could say anything at all and not be judged for it. We could express any feeling, doubt, question or opinion without reprimand, rebuke or rejection. This was as refreshing as an oasis to a stranded desert traveller. The nature of the religion is that you cannot express serious doubts or question without fear of being labelled a troublemaker or 'weak in the faith'. The results of vocalising doubts or questioning the leadership's wisdom are evident; people drift away from you, whilst labelling you a 'bad associate', 'independent thinker', or even something severe as a 'wolf in sheep's clothing' or 'Apostate' (the ultimate in evil as far as a Witness is concerned). With Jake I had no such fears and was in essence free to speak my mind, a great release of contained pressures.

Please don't think that I am equating a great friendship to a mere tool of self-therapy. It served and continues to serve as such, but of course is so much more. We were 'spiritual brothers' but have become more like real brothers, prepared to go further than even Jehovah's Witnesses would give themselves praise for, in aid of the other.

CHAPTER 4

LIFE AS A WITNESS

MY ESCAPE

"To the Body of Elders,

This letter is to advise you that I cannot accept the Watchtower Corporation as God's sole channel of communication nor his faithful slave, nor his spirit directed organisation. As you are aware, there are significant elements in its history where claims were made regarding dates and Armageddon. These along with numerous other incorrect teachings all serve to indicate that the Watchtower could not possibly be the ones providing 'food at the proper time', nor the organisation chosen by Christ in 1918 as is believed (currently).

To add to the worry these things cause is the 'playing down' of such errors, some of which were also blamed on the brothers for 'reading into' things too much. The most recent of these would seem to be 1975. Watchtower articles blamed the brothers for expecting Armageddon when no such expectation was warranted.

Yet the titles and articles gave more than an indication that the time of the end was due for imminent conclusion in 1975. Articles headed 'Why Are You Looking Forward To 1975?' and convention badges entitled 'Who Will Conquer The World In The 1970s?' are strong evidence of this. This is just one example from a plethora of documented inconsistencies and false teachings that were later changed, some of which I brought to your attention previously. Should this letter reach the branch office then they should be fully aware of these already.

On the subject of my position as one of Jehovah's Witnesses I must explain an issue that has become apparent only recently. Firstly, I was raised as a follower as you are aware and got baptised some 6-7 years ago. Interestingly, I was not aware at any point (until a few weeks ago) that a person is to make a personal dedication to God before baptism. Having never made such a dedication my baptism should be viewed as null and void, and I maintain a clear conscience, having broken no vow to God. Neither disfellowshipping nor disassociation would grant me the freedom to continue my life without significant damage to the relationship I hold with both my mother and my brother (who is in desperate need of my attention and companionship). I am fully aware of the practice of shunning former members and find it disturbing that whilst this is enforced, something quite contrary is being printed:

July 2009 Awake! p29: "No one should be forced to worship in a way that he finds unacceptable or be made to choose between his beliefs and his family."

I can plainly state now that my decision to get baptised was not an informed one, as had I known of the magnitude and quantity of changed teachings and failed prophesies in the past and recent history of the Watchtower, I most certainly would not have maintained association for as long as I have.

Whilst I can easily say that the average witness is generally a decent person with strong moral courage, I cannot make the same comment with regards to a system that controls the lives of so many and disregards the responsibility of the consequences of their rules and regulations, and holds a person to ransom for fear of losing their family.

Yours, in all sincerity

Anthony James"

The above letter is something I never could have dreamt would come from my own hand, yet here it is. How I got to this point will now be examined.

We had been moved back into our former home, now refurbished, and with the derelict, scorched shell of a home still attached. It was a constant reminder of the horrors we had faced, and it would be months before a developer rebuilt it. This aside, we were trying to settle and move on with our lives, though I was still struggling with my low sense of wellbeing and conflicting beliefs. I had been offered counselling, but declined, feeling that talking wouldn't solve anything. In addition no one, I felt, could handle or help me with what had plagued me so deeply. I wasn't prepared to readily offload the deepest feelings that I had guarded to just anyone. I had tried anti-depressant medication, which hadn't really served its purpose. Life was a task of endurance, with the only enjoyment being time spent with my little brother, my best friend Jake, or sleeping.

My time spent on the ministry work had dwindled to near non-existence, and my meeting attendance had become less and less. People naturally started to notice, and before long a plan was hatched to offer me encouragement. Normally the Elders in the congregation would initiate this, as it is their responsibility to care for the 'flock of God'. Before this plan was put into action however, I found a new hobby, one that helped Jake, my brother, and myself: magic. This new pastime was exciting, challenging, and engaging. Whilst called magic, everyone who has a brain between his or her ears knows it is purely a trick, simply an optical illusion. Nevertheless, I would soon receive constant pressure from the Elders to stop this harmless activity. After a short while, Jake and I formed an entertainment business, which has been very successful.

Before I had launched it as a career, I had an opportunity to show some Witnesses my new skills at a small gathering at a Brother and Sister's home. The performance went well, and it was very enjoyable for all present, up until one moment. One of the Sisters suddenly said, "Show me the six of hearts". It was a rather outstanding moment when I cleanly and openly placed my empty hand into my pocket and withdrew a single card: the six of hearts. The room went deadly silent. I casually tossed the card to the table, giving it a slight spin for effect. The reality was that I had placed that particular card in my pocket before leaving the house, planning to use it for a trick later. It was a complete coincidence that she named that card, yet I had a visit from an Elder that week pleading with me to stop doing magic. The belief was that I was in league with demons and was using some kind of psychological suggestion or similar to control the minds of others. The Brother had printed out Watchtower articles and scriptures aimed at this subject. He also begged me to stop my friendship with Jake, calling him a bad influence. Everything that gave me relief from the misery that was my life was under attack. I was being pressured to give up the very things that were keeping me going. It was at this moment the penny dropped, so to speak. It struck me that people are so willing to believe in certain things that they will readily suspend logical thought processes to accept a supernatural explanation in an instant. After all it was just a card trick (and to tell the truth, I wasn't even that good back then), yet they still believed.

My thoughts had begun to wonder about other aspects of life. If a room full of Jehovah's Witnesses could believe I was demonic for something so simple, what other things are believed without adequate evidence?

As I learned more and more magical effects, taught by some of the world's finest sleight of hand experts in books and DVDs, I discovered something that cemented my previous thought. No matter how impressive and amazing a magical effect was, there ALWAYS was a simple and more importantly natural method behind the effect. To Jake and myself it had become almost comical that certain individuals had started to avoid us, fearing demonic influence. Others weren't so naïve, but the Elders were still trying to get me to stop. We were however going in the opposite direction, having recently secured a deal with a local restaurant to perform on Friday and Saturday evenings in exchange for food and drink. Despite not receiving money for our work, we gained masses of experience and proof that we were capable, and could look to charge for our services. At last I had something exciting to be proud of, a skill that few others had. It was something that made for interesting conversations, and could break the ice in almost any situation. The pressure from the Elders to stop only achieved one thing; it pushed me further away from 'the truth', and in their eyes into Satan's grasp. Their last attempt to thwart my promising career was to bring up how evil deception is and to quote scriptures. Their aim to use fear to bring me to their way of thinking:

> "...those who are disgusting in their filth and murderers and fornicators and those practicing spiritism and idolaters and all the liars, their portion will be in the lake that burns with fire and sulphur." - *Revelation 21:8*.

Alas I would sit, listen and nod in apparent agreement, but do absolutely nothing to comply with their requests. It must have been frustrating for them if nothing else. I was not going to throw away the few things that were keeping me from giving up on life. I was reaching suffocation point with regards to the pressures I was feeling on the inside, and those that were being applied from the outside by the Elders and others. Mum had been quietly and consistently supporting me, never criticising, just caring for me by means of encouragement. I couldn't tell her what or how I was really feeling, as I knew it would break her heart. She must have had some idea though, and had asked for an experienced Brother to have a Bible study with me. The aim of course was to rebuild my faith and bring me back to Jehovah. I went along and over the course of a few months studied with the kind Brother. He remarked to Mum how impressed he was with my scriptural knowledge and power of reasoning. However, he was saddened by the fact that he could not get me to open up. As I said beforehand, my personal feelings were protected, though perhaps this was self-damaging. I would not reveal them until I was ready and happy with whom I was speaking to. Not to say this man wasn't warm and gentle, but I just couldn't do it.

It was at this time I had begun to research the theory of evolution. I had previously had many discussions with a non-Witness at work and had doggedly stuck to the notion that it was plain nonsense. Now however I was a little more open minded, and was determined to prove to myself that there was either a creator or there wasn't. Technically speaking, evolutionary theory has nothing to do with whether there is a god or not, but as Jehovah's Witnesses firmly reject it, I would learn something nonetheless. When I mentioned to Mum that I wanted to learn about this subject, she pointed me towards the Watchtower Society's books and magazines as the source of information I should be using. This is after all where Witnesses derive most of their knowledge, favouring it over 'man's fallible efforts'. When I said no to that, she urged me to look at "non biased" information that examined "both sides". I said no to this too stating that I had 20 + years of biased information driven into my brain, and I wanted to hear the undiluted hard evidence from the other side. As I started to actually research the subject I came to realise that I actually knew nothing about how evolution works. I was astonished. For years I thought that Evolution was one of my specialist subjects. The reality that became evident was that I used arguments that I now know are utterly asinine.

I used to argue with ignorant reasoning that to my fellow brethren and myself made perfect sense. They were things like:

Life is too complicated to have evolved

Why don't we see monkeys turning into people today?

Everything in the universe including us couldn't have come from nothing

Why don't we see 'in between' species forming?

The universe is too 'finely tuned' to have arisen by accident

Having slowly gained an education in real scientific and rational thinking, I began to see the fallacies that had made up much of my belief system.

It was during this stage in my life that an opportunity to move out of the house and a little further away from the religion's grip arose. I moved into a large three-bedroom house with Jake and his 'worldly' (non-Witness) girlfriend. The house we found was just down the road, in the centre of the village. Having made the announcement to Mum, who was probably less thrilled than she let on, I commenced making necessary plans for the move. It would turn out to be very hard on my little brother, who was very sad to see me go, having spent his whole life growing up with me.

Mum made an effort to perhaps dissuade me from making the move by extolling the potential implications. She reasoned with me that although I was not going to many meetings, I was still a baptised Brother. This meant I could expect the possibility of disciplinary action by the Elders of the congregation if I went ahead with the move. What was the reason for this? Well, Jake was in a relationship with his non-Witness girlfriend. This was highly frowned upon. Their moving in together technically should have prompted the Elders to hold a 'Judicial Hearing'. Should Jake not have wished to change his living arrangement, they would decide without evidence, that he was guilty of having a sexual relationship out-of-wedlock. They would therefore remove him from the congregation by means of disfellowshipping. This meant that none of his Witness friends or family would speak to him ever, at all. Not even a smile or acknowledgement should they pass him in the street. However, Jake had moved house several times within the previous two years. He was technically in another congregation, and therefore under their jurisdiction. As he was now going to be living in my congregation's territory, he seemed to be largely left alone. Where I factored into this was simply 'guilt by association'. By living in the same house I would be condoning their actions. This would be seen as a lowering of God's standards. To be honest though, I really didn't care. I knew all this already and was planning to move regardless.

Aside from a case of last minute jitters from myself, the move went according to plan and a whole new world had opened up to me. As well as having my own room and personal space, I now had to do more for myself.

I would make it to the occasional Witness meeting but ultimately was planning to stop attending altogether. I eventually reached breaking point with my willpower to go to these desperately uninteresting and unfulfilling gatherings. Despite the 'niceness' of the association beforehand and afterwards, the general content seemed simply to be a regurgitation of the same old information over and over. Now that I didn't have the frequent, gentle, but life-draining invitations from Mum before each and every meeting, I could breathe just that little bit more. In my absence I could almost hear the chatter at the Kingdom Hall, as inevitably there would be considerable talk about me. This would most probably range from concerned casual gossip all the way up to discussion at Elder's meetings. People talk - Witnesses more than most.

With my new living space I had more time to reflect on life, along with the freedom to study the two subjects that particularly interested me: Evolution and the history of the Watchtower Society (both will be examined in following chapters). I had to be sure of what was really true and what wasn't. If what I had been brought up to believe was the truth, then it should have been easy to restore the faith I once had.

With my troubled body and mind I had been prescribed medication for anxiety, which was seen to be the cause of my ailments. This new treatment enabled me to restore a large portion of my function, and I was now able to cope far better with day-to-day activities, including work. The constant state of feeling ill had largely been reduced which gave me the ability to start to enjoy things again, although I would still have a fight on my hands (there are few quick fixes in this life). If I were to put a percentage on how well I was feeling, it would be somewhere in the region of 60%, whilst on the medication. This was pretty good, having felt as low as 10-20% at my worst, and averaging 30-40% on 'good days' before. My Cognitive Behavioural Therapist (CBT) gave me this scoring idea. I began the therapy, which was conducted via telephone shortly after I started taking the new medication. I must confess that I'm not convinced it helped me that much. This was partly due to my almost clichéd male approach, which of course meant I would not fully open up during the sessions. As kind as she was as a therapist, I was only just about able to talk about the pressure I was feeling from the Jehovah's Witnesses. I was also sad about the disappointment I knew that Mum felt. She must have been equally, if not more upset with herself, seeing a failure in the mirror each time she prepared to go to the meeting (alone). My sister had drifted away from meetings a year or more before myself. She however had not got baptised, which meant she did not face any judicial action or shunning.

What must have also hurt Mum is that my brother was dragging his heels when it came to attending the meetings. She had gone from having a relatively stable family unit, to in some sense losing it all. The loss of dad was total, though she believed she would see him again in the New

System upon his resurrection. My sister had stopped going to meetings and had a boyfriend who, despite being kind, positive, and an all-round good person, was not a Witness. There were few signs that they were going to come into 'the truth'. I was also heading away from the religion that was her whole life; as a result her perceived failure was complete.

Another pressure I felt was that of the disappointment of everyone in the congregation. All the people I had viewed as family for all those years, and had worked with on the ministry, or socialised with at gatherings, would of course feel a deep sadness for my 'falling away' from 'the truth'. I know this because I myself had felt such sadness when others had drifted away, and I had seen and heard others express similar feelings. Mum had previously said that I had become highly respected in the congregation, and it was possible that one day I could have been an Elder. I had gone from being a beacon of potential to a stray and lost soul.

I was also feeling a lot of pressure from my employer. At every possible opportunity he would make a comment to urge me to come back to meetings. This really took its toll on me, but I didn't have the backbone to tell him to stop. I would simply grin and bear the torturous barrage of accumulated pressure. I would also have to sit in earshot, as each and every representative from suppliers would be told the same story of how the global system was at the brink of total collapse. This fear-inducing speech was concluded with the description of how Jehovah is going to step in and annihilate the wicked people of the world, which includes everyone who is not a Jehovah's Witness. This cumulative influence massively hindered my progress in drifting away from 'the truth'.

Some time later, I made a huge step by asking a girl out on a date. I had always been lousy at talking to girls and never got anywhere, which was not helped by the strict courtship rules that Witnesses adhere to. Men and women who are unmarried are not allowed to spend any time alone together. This is simply because they cannot be trusted not to have sexual contact, therefore chaperones are required at all times. How someone is to make a proper judgement regarding suitability of a partner without spending any time alone with them is frankly baffling. Without these same restrictions I could more freely and openly look for love. At first I was unsure of where to start, but social media came to the rescue. Having narrowed my sites onto one particular girl that I had known when I was a child, I looked for an opportunity to gauge any possible interest on her part. She happened to announce that she was going to be at a craft fayre in the village, selling bits and pieces. I decided to go along and say hello. We had not spoken since childhood, despite going to the same secondary school. Both our mums knew each other and they had been casual friends for a good number of years. I somewhat nervously walked into the small hall where the craft fayre was being held. I tried to 'play it cool' (which I think I pulled off pretty successfully) and didn't show any signs of particular interest. I stayed for about twenty minutes and bought a couple of bits and pieces from her stall. It was quite nice to catch up a little and I left thinking there might be a possibility of something more developing. I was not holding on to too much hope though, as in the past I had let my feelings get ahead of the reality of the situation. It was a strange feeling though, I was doing what I wanted to do with my life, but there was an element of guilt at play. I was running a course that went against everything I had previously stood for. My feelings were playing against me at this point. I had subtle undertones of guilt that came from thinking about what Mum would think should she find out, though in many ways it must have been inevitable that I would eventually take this course. I also wondered that if the Witness beliefs were true, my dad would be resurrected to a world where I had not made it through. The feelings that worked their way into my subconscious as a result of these thoughts presented themselves as added stress in addition to guilt.

I resolved however, that until I discover to my satisfaction the truth about the universe and the existence of a creator, I would live my life according to my decisions. I could not go back to following the excessively demanding rules and regulations that Watchtower Society required of its followers. My head was still in a mess though, with all of this back-and-forth thinking plaguing my conscious mind. I still was very unsettled, with thoughts and fears that I may have made a grave mistake, and that Armageddon would come and I would have failed right at the crucial moment. This was pure torture at times, with my rationality fighting against indoctrinated fear and programmed thought patterns. The fight continued...

My determination would not be easily defeated though. With that I made the bold step and asked Imogen out on a date. It was a week or so later that she responded, during which time I guessed she was not interested. However, she said yes to my request and we made plans to go out for pizza. Having secured a time where I could talk one-on-one with a girl for the first time in my entire life, I was, to say the least, a little nervous. I was determined to be smart though and therefore viewed the evening as a casual affair, which alleviated much of the pressure and I was able to be myself. We talked and joked whilst enjoying our meal. I was impressed how she spoke openly to me and like an actual human being. Something I never really experienced when talking to girls in the congregation. I don't know how to really explain what I mean, but I felt that Witness girls weren't interested in talking to me. Imogen was different because she talked and listened. She smiled, and laughed without any suggestion of being fake. It was not until our second date that the inevitable topic came up. She asked if I was still a Witness and upon my negative response sighed in relief. She openly stated it would have been a 'deal-breaker' for her, and she would not be able to continue seeing me. We sat and talked about what I believed now and why. She had heard of what the family had been through recently and was kind and empathetic, which quickly built my trust in her.

We continued to see each other and our romance blossomed over the following weeks. There was unease on my part though when we went out together. I was afraid of being seen out with a girl. The repercussions that could follow were potentially grave. Should people find out, the Elders could subject me to judicial action, which could include disfellowshipping. This would mean that no Witnesses would be permitted to even speak to me, including my mother. When we walked down the street together I would shy away from holding hands, and was frequently looking over my shoulder. I knew eventually it would become known, but why accelerate the arrival of a difficult and unpleasant hurdle? After a short while however I decided I must get something out of the way. I needed to tell Mum about Imogen. I knew in many ways it would make her sad, and so I couldn't face her to tell her. I decided to write a short letter explaining my change in circumstances. I wasn't sure what to expect after she read it. Fortunately however she wasn't as outraged or distraught as I had feared. Rather she was actually quite kind, saying that my choice of partner was about as good as she could have asked for, second only to a Witness of course. That was a relief, but I knew there would be trouble ahead in one shape or another. The only question was when.

One thing that I knew to be true was that word travels fast in the close-knit community that makes up each congregation. It didn't take long for people to start asking questions and I had of course to respond with an affirmative answer. There was no point in lying, even if I wanted to. Once I knew that it was more or less common knowledge amongst the Witnesses I relaxed a little when out with Imogen, fearing a little less about being seen than I had. However I would not completely relax until much later. I was still worried about seeing any congregation members while at the shops or in the street. I didn't want to have to talk to them, as I had largely differing views now and knew the effect their seemingly innocent remarks may have on me. Inside me lay deeply entrenched and almost hard-wired thought patterns that could be triggered by any number of things. Just seeing a Brother or Sister again would trigger overwhelming feelings of guilt and shame. I knew how I would have viewed people who were in my shoes when I was still an active Witness. I was just trying to stay away from it all. I didn't want them to see me, think of me, speak of me, and especially not come for me. Deep down however, I knew they would.

Whilst I was away from the Kingdom Hall, I was in the dark with respect to changes, gossip and other activities that previously occupied so much of my time. It wasn't long however before something happened. I was eating dinner one evening with Jake and his girlfriend when two Elders arrived at our door, dressed in suits with Bibles in hand. This was a completely unexpected visit. Neither of them had the courtesy to call me beforehand to arrange a meeting, despite having my number. They asked to come in, which I allowed. We sat in the living room and the conversation, as I would soon learn would always start with general pleasantries and chitchat. After a few minutes they got down to what they really came for. They claimed to have '...heard through the grapevine...' that I now had a girlfriend who was not a Witness. Once I acknowledged that this was indeed the case they asked a little about her, things like where we met, what she did for work etc. The next line of questioning was entirely personal. They stated that it puts them in a position where they need to look at the 'cleanliness of the congregation'. As I was '...still technically a Witness', I may have been bringing the congregation (and therefore Jehovah) into disrepute. They then stated plainly, 'We need to know if you're having sex'. This was an unbelievably inappropriate question that completely took me by surprise. Knowing what was at stake, I immediately replied that I most certainly was not, irrespective of the reality. I was furious that they thought they had the right to know what I was, or wasn't doing with my genitalia, but couldn't muster the courage to tell them to leave. Such is the power they had over me. Shortly after this point however, they did leave, having asked the only question they actually cared about, and having unsuccessfully tried to also talk to Jake. There was a distinct difference in reaction from Jake and myself though. I had allowed them to come into our home and interrogate me. I had given them a considerable level of power over me, without realising it. My subservience had been an automatic response to seeing them. They still had the power to take away my believing family by telling them to shun me, and I was afraid of this. In addition, they had always had authority over me whilst growing up, and my immediate reaction upon seeing them again was to view them the same way. This visit felt more official than 'just a chat'. I knew I was doing something wrong in my life, at least from their viewpoint, which was also still deeply rooted into my own subconscious and all added to the pressure felt.

I was affected for days by this visit. They had turned up unannounced, demanding to know the most intimate details of my life. What was this the start of? I was already battling stress, anxiety, and apparent illness. Why was there now this added strain? I didn't hear from them until after my situation changed again a few months later.

Things with Imogen had been going very well and we had decided to take another big step in our relationship and move in together. She was living at home and wanted a place of her own. I wanted to spend more time with her, so it wasn't long before we were looking for somewhere to live and began buying bits and pieces in preparation for our new home. We found a nice small flat in the village that was comfortably within our budget and things were set in motion. When I told Mum, I don't think she was too surprised, but was worried that it would make things more difficult for her as she would face a challenge to her loyalty. She said that as I was living in a way that was disapproved by Jehovah; she would never be able to come round for a meal and must be careful how and when she associated with me. Any association that wasn't strictly a family emergency would be seen as condoning our unacceptable behaviour. I knew all this already, but it was difficult to hear the words as they left her mouth. I could tell it was hurting her to say them. In reality it was a somewhat speculative conversation, warning me of what *might* have to happen. During this conversation we also discussed briefly some of the reasons why I was having trouble with 'the truth'. These included some of the things I had learned about the history of the religion along with my more recent findings in the study of evolution. She didn't like what I was saying and even denied some of the historical facts that I disclosed. I simply told her to look them up for herself if she was unsure. I left it at that, not wishing to push any further.

Having resolved to carry on with my plans to move in with Imogen (somewhat regardless of the consequences), I continued collecting bits and pieces for our new place. To my surprise, Mum even purchased some things for us, which was nice. I chose to view this as her desire to see me happy, for which I am both glad and grateful. On the one hand she was a devout follower and believer in the faith that had encapsulated so much of our lives. On the other, she was a human being, with natural maternal feelings. In addition, perhaps she hoped that these kindnesses would somehow encourage me to come back to the faith. I assume the reality was a combination of these factors. It was nice not to be totally rejected, which I feared would be the case, knowing the religion's rules regarding these matters. It was a pleasant relief that she hadn't taken the harshest of stands, instead choosing a more moderate one.

I was at this point enjoying the new experience of living in my own place, with my lovely girlfriend. Not having the massively demanding schedule that the religion requires its followers to adhere to was letting me explore new hobbies and interests whilst undertaking a journey of self-discovery. Imogen was incredibly supportive and encouraging during this period, and was helping me as I battled to adjust my viewpoint on the world. There was much adjustment needed, as I had to try to undo more than twenty years of heavy indoctrination. This process would take a long time, perhaps many years, yet it had become my quest. I still wasn't settled on my beliefs. My logical thinking process was telling me that none of what I had believed in was true and the science backed this up, BUT the fear was still present. What if I was wrong? I had to be sure, and therefore continued my research, collecting information, evidence, and more logical points of reasoning. It was a wholly unnatural process, trying to accept a belief system that I had viciously rejected for my entire life, and at the same time trying to break down the old one that had been so deeply rooted (yet was clearly flawed). Coming to terms with a realisation that there is not an all-loving creator with an army of angels, and a devil with an army of demons, was not easy. Accepting the mountain of evidence for evolution (see chapter seven), a concept I had ridiculed as a Witness was easy for the logical part of my brain. Letting it replace the flawed, unfounded, yet hard-wired previous model would be a painful task. Relinquishing the belief and desire for the New System, the problem free paradise that I had both craved and prayed for, was the literal abandonment of a dream.

One of the points I developed during my extensive contemplation was a realisation that God *did* have a choice when judging Adam and Eve. My Witness-trained viewpoint was that God had no alternative but to remove the gift of perfection and everlasting life from the rebellious couple. He could not simply destroy the 'wicked' pair and start again, for this would only prove his power and not his right to rule mankind. When Satan teased Eve, he (according to the Witness beliefs) was both calling God a liar, and questioning his sovereignty. He was 'effectively' saying that we (humans) had the right to rule ourselves. By eating the forbidden fruit, Adam sinned (Eve's sin didn't really matter as she was a woman) and mirrored the view that Satan had allegedly asserted. A bite of fruit was a rejection of God, a demand to be free from his rule. It was a demand that he had readily granted.

Once my mind was able to process this concept without the bombardment of Watchtower information, I could dissect it and align it against my own sense of right and wrong. It quickly fell apart, starting with the fruit-test. With a paradise world created, and two humans settled and instructed to fill the earth, a single restriction was placed on them. The tree was named 'the tree of knowledge of good and bad' which I began to realise was an utterly questionable choice of name, and apparently incredibly tempting as *"...the woman saw that the fruit of the tree was good for food and pleasing to the eye..."* (Genesis 3:6). God, being a gallant soul had made the prohibited fruit particularly appealing, especially to Eve. This was coupled by the appearance of the talking snake, whose voice was none other than Satan. His lie fooled Eve into eating the fruit, and Adam (who according to scripture, was with her) ate it too. Jehovah God being all-knowing would of course have been watching the whole thing unfold. I question why he would allow the rebellious angel Satan to take control of a snake, and deceive his latest project into breaking the only law he had laid out, resulting in their deaths, and untold future suffering. Seeing as the first human couple would have never been exposed to a lie, how would they be expected to question what they were being told? Also, did they have a real understanding of what death was? The Bible does not say whether animals had eternal life back then. However it does say *"...by one man sin entered into the world, and death by sin; and so death passed upon all men, for that all have sinned."* (Romans 5:12). If death entered the world through man's sin, then death could not have been present previously. Quite how this allows for the extinction of the dinosaurs remains to be explained. If Adam and Eve had no understanding of the reality of death, how could they respect the seriousness of the rule not to eat of the tree?

The very name of the tree indicates that if one were to consume its produce, a new level of understanding would be granted, much in the way the Devil described. A particular human characteristic is the quest for further knowledge and understanding. It's what has got us so far technologically, and so it would appear an 'easy sell' for Satan. The key illustration used by Witnesses is derived from the 'teacher – student' analogy (discussed in chapter one). My main problem with this whole situation is God's decision to let Adam and Eve die slowly and allowing them to bare children, who would also have death ingrained in their destiny. If it was the case that Adam deserved death for his crime, why not execute him as promised and start afresh? By creating a new pair, mankind could avoid the millennia of pain and suffering that has wrought misery upon countless billions of people throughout history. The explanation given is that God had intended for Adam's seed to fill the earth and therefore had no choice but to leave them to it. He made a plan for mankind's redemption however, by the arrival on earth of his son Jesus who would be executed to balance the scales and allow God to forgive mankind for the original offence. The spilling of Jesus' perfect blood would appease God's wrath (only for those who believe and worship him). As a believer, this is seen as a loving provision. However now it appears a sadistic self-serving egotistical exercise. The author Richard Dawkins summed it up quite well when he said, "If God wanted to forgive our sins, why not just forgive them?" How true that is when you factor in the seemingly endless suffering that has and continues to go on throughout the Earth. To what end? To prove that man cannot rule himself? Not when we're imperfect we can't. Change that variable, and I'll bet we could give it a go.

Additionally I would argue that it is both unloving and immoral to have the means to end such suffering, yet choose to delay. If I were to see a child suffering to the point of dying and I did nothing but watch, you would think me a monster. Even if it was the child's own foolishness that got them into trouble in the first place. Choosing not to act just to prove a point to a third party (in this case Satan) is wholly unacceptable and to my mind as cruel or unloving as I can imagine. Allowing such abject suffering whilst being quite capable of ending or even preventing it, is only marginally less evil than being the direct cause, which I argue he was. The famous quote, "All that is necessary for the triumph of evil is that good men do nothing" springs to mind.

Furthermore, by granting Satan first a voice, then direct influence in the situation, God fell right into his trap. Now Jehovah is playing along with Satan's game. Why would a supreme being give an unqualified, undeserving, and clearly capricious individual a chance to ruin his project, knowing what was at stake. If the Bible is to be believed, God has the power to see into the future. He could therefore not just guess what was going to happen; he could see it before it unfolded. As the angels apparently were witnesses to this issue, could Jehovah not have shown them a vision of what would take place and let the angels decide for themselves who was right and who was wrong? Satan should have been executed or imprisoned for his rebellion as soon as he told the first lie to Eve. But no, God allowed it all, and Satan would not receive his due punishment until after the thousand-year reign, after Armageddon. For some reason he will also be allowed a last period of rule to drag as many people to the lake of fire and sulphur with him. Where is the love and justice in any of this? What's more, God even chooses to punish the snake that was possessed by Satan: *"So the LORD God said to the serpent, "Because you have done this, cursed are you above all livestock and all wild animals! You will crawl on your belly and you will eat dust all the days of your life."* (Genesis 3:14). What did the snake do to deserve any such punishment? This whole fiasco can be seen for what it truthfully is, utter nonsense.

This realisation was a key point in developing my own critical thinking skills. I was really starting to assess things for myself. If something was right, it was no longer because God said so. I still had a long way to go though, and challenges unlike Armageddon were just around the corner. I received a few messages from concerned Brothers and Sisters, to whom I replied that I was having some problems with 'the truth'. One individual in particular took it upon himself to put to rest the issues I was having. When I sent him over a short list of things that troubled me about the Watchtower Society, he went away and did some research. He came back with ultimate dismissal, claiming the society had either done no wrong, or if there were questionable actions or beliefs they were corrected as 'new light' was shone on the situation. The former Watchtower Governing Body member Raymond Franz further justified my issues when I read his book 'Crisis of Conscience'. He described how things really worked at the Witness headquarters. They were a far stretch from how things are portrayed in Watchtower literature, and further still from the idyllic way I had pictured, and would hear described from the platform at the Kingdom Hall. This will be examined in chapters five and seven.

It clearly didn't take long for the Elders to discover that I wasn't merely drifting away, but was digging up information that they'd rather not have spread about. My boss had a meeting with me where he warned that the Circuit Overseer was due for a visit to our congregation. He warned that it would be likely I would be approached because of my living situation. He urged me to approach the Elders beforehand and repent for my sins, claiming it would look far better than if they had to 'come and get me'. I said I'd think about it, but of course had no intention of running back, especially after learning what I had. This kind of pressure I felt day in and day out, whether anything was said or not. I could feel the disapproval, despite my best efforts to be the best I could be at my work. There was a break of a couple of weeks before anything happened, and I figured that maybe it was just a scare tactic to get me to come back, and the Elders were not really interested in me. As it happens, I was wrong.

It was an uncanny case of timing as I was standing at a bar with Jake and he happened to say something along the lines of "Have you heard anything from them then?" I got out my phone, looked at the time and said "Well it won't be tonight as it's a meeting night and it's 7pm - they'll be all arriving at the Kingdom Hall.". Literally as I uttered those words with my phone in my hand, it started to ring. Knowing the Elder who was calling, I decided to answer it. He said that he was just wondering how I was and wanted to meet up for a chat to 'catch up'. I said I would be happy to, but thought it just as easy to do it over the phone. He said that he had trouble with his hearing and would find it easier if we could indeed meet at his house. I agreed, partly out of interest but also out of the programmed submissiveness that made saying no nearly impossible. I didn't really want to see him, but at that point simply couldn't refuse, particularly due to the friendly yet coercive manner in which it was conveyed.

When the day came for the arranged meeting, I walked up to the house with Imogen. She walked back leaving me to enter a house I had never imagined I would set foot in again. Upon being greeted at the door, I walked into the living room where there was another Elder. This was it! I was not expecting to have another Elder present and the only reason this would be the case is the requirement for two witnesses to any accusation or admission of wrongdoing. Suddenly it became evident that the claim that a hearing problem was the reason for a face to face meeting was at best a half truth, at worst an outright lie. The usual friendly chitchat was to prelude the real reason why they had lured me in. They questioned my living situation, which I answered honestly. They then asked me that question once again regarding my sexual activity, which I immediately denied. Once again, from where do they get this idea that they have the right to know in any case? When have I demanded that information from them? Alas, they seemed to have acquired enough information and said right at the end that they would just need to inform the other Elders. Now the other Elders are involved. It was supposed to be a friendly one-to-one catch-up, but clearly that was never the case. I had said during the meeting that I didn't view myself as a Witness and was not interested in staying in touch with any of them (therefore would not be jeopardising their consciences, nor the 'cleanliness of the congregation'). I had also said that my critical concern was the wellbeing of my brother. Having spent so much time together and been through what we had, I was like a dad to him. They had the power to potentially take him away from me, by disfellowshipping me. Mum would be expected to prevent him from ever seeing me; at least until he was an adult, at which time he would be able to choose for himself. If he wanted to be a Jehovah's Witness then he would too have to shun me.

I wanted to make clear that I was not going to be a pushover however, and had prepared a list of the main things I had learned about the Watchtower Society; particularly its history, which had troubled me. They glanced at the list briefly, saying that they had heard of some of them, but not most. I said to them that I was deeply stumbled by these things and welcomed their response after they had time to check them out. This however they did not do. The next call I received was a request that I come in for a judicial hearing. I was disappointed by this as I'd appealed to them to respond to these issues, which as far as they were concerned may have brought me back into 'the truth'.

Imogen accompanied me to the judicial hearing, which was held at the Kingdom Hall. She waited in the car as I went in. We went into a back room where I would alone face the inquisition of three Elders, as no people acting as support or witnesses are permitted on the side of the accused. The initial part of this meeting lasted for an hour, during which we talked mostly about my living situation where, instead of asking if I was having a sexual relationship, they assumed it to be the case. I had to interject and state that the scripture they were using to 'convict' me didn't apply, as I was not in fact engaging in 'immorality'. I had a fight to get them to admit that it meant I was therefore not to be charged for that reason. They begrudgingly did, but it didn't matter, they were intent on the predetermined outcome. One point the main Elder made was that the purpose of the judicial hearing was not to establish guilt, but repentance. I said that if I was not guilty, then I had nothing to repent for. I also stated that as far as I was concerned I was not a Jehovah's Witness anymore, but needed the situation to remain the same so that I could continue to see my brother whose welfare would suffer if he were cut off from me. At the time they simply nodded, as if to say that it was my fault that is was the case. At no point did they even mention the issues I had raised, nor did they do or say anything to refute me when I gave them schooling on the theory of evolution. I explained how the Watchtower had utterly miss-taught the theory using creationist pseudo-science. This information fell on deaf ears.

After the initial hour I was asked to leave for the three Elders to have a private discussion. I went and sat in the car with Imogen. They spent half an hour seemingly deciding my fate and I was hedging my bets at this point. At the time, if I were given the choice I would rather remain a Witness officially and have the freedom to see my brother and mother. If they would just let me drift away from 'the truth' there would be no problems. I had written the letter of disassociation days before and had it in my back pocket should I feel it appropriate to give to them. I knew at this point that there was so much wrong with the religion, that it could not possibly be 'the truth'. I was sick of the power they had over my family and me, and the fear they could instil in me if I saw any of them. The dread of such which had been a source of frequent anxiety. Once they had concluded their discussion, one of them came outside to fetch me. I sat down once again and was greeted with the news that I was to be disfellowshipped. It was both a blessing and a curse. On the positive side, a huge sigh of relief could be had. A large chapter of my life could be closed, with much of my anxiety duly put to rest. This moment I had dreaded had come and gone, and now I was officially free. However I now had to face Mum with the news and see where she drew her line. Would she cut me off entirely as the religion demanded, or would she let me still be her son? Time would tell, but for the moment I had to look on the bright side. As I got up to leave I mentioned that I had written a summary of my thoughts and feelings and would like the Elders to read them. I handed them the copy from my pocket, and they said they would read it now before showing it to the rest of the Elders. They stated that the door was always open for me to come back should I be prepared to change my ways. My unspoken response was 'unlikely mate', or something similar. As I got into the car I simply uttered to Imogen, "Well, I'm out", and we drove home, both excited and nervous. This prolonged torturous affair had gone on long enough, and Imogen had been burdened with more than she deserved, as had I.

Where the crutch of my concern now lay was purely how Mum would react. She can't have expected me to merely turn on the waterworks and submit in a defeatist fashion to the authoritarian committee that was targeting me, as I had heard of so many doing before. I know she longed for me to return to the faith. This was as saddening for me as I imagine it must be for her. She must have known it was coming, and had even suggested I say to the Elders that I was having a few problems with 'the truth' and needed some time to work out where I was. She hoped I could buy some time and maintain the status quo, leaving the need for further action for a later time. It was too late for that and I was now officially out, cut off from all the people I had viewed as my large family, my only friends. They would now be tested if they saw me. What would they do? Their instruction is not to greet me, smile at me, or even acknowledge my existence. I am to be dead to them, until I return to the flock, having seen the error of my ways.

So far however my mother has been as good as I could expect under the circumstances. I know the pressure she is under not to speak to me, but she so far has not cut me out of her life. She has taken small steps to limit the association we share, but I trust she can see that family is truly important in life. Should she come to read this one day, then I hope she understands that this writing is an expression of all the things I could not say. It is also a reality check, as there is much about the religion that goes unsaid, unknown, or is untruthfully expressed. The view from any Jehovah's Witness who by chance come to hear about this book will claim it a piece of Apostate propaganda, a tool of Satan, or the words of a bitter or misguided fool. They would not read it, nor ever even open it for fear of damaging their faith. My questions to any such ones are simply these: If you have the truth, what are you afraid of? Is it so weak that it cannot withstand criticism? Do you not trust yourself to judge information accordingly?

One interesting point that I brought out in my letter to the Elders was the fact that although I got baptised, I made no dedication to God. Whilst I now see the likelihood of the existence of any such celestial being to be minimal at best, from their point of view I had turned my back on God. I wanted to be sure that they knew that from my viewpoint I should be exempt from shunning and my baptism was void. However the Elders seemingly ignored this and have marked me to be avoided by all. I have experienced being ignored at work by many Witnesses who visit. Some have broken the rules and spoken to me, albeit briefly, but most will avoid me wherever possible. This is not entirely negative however. Previously it was I who walked the streets in fear, looking over my shoulder. Now, they hide from me, and I travel without apprehension. The tables have turned, so to speak, and they are the ones now in a minority. I have an ever-expanding group of friends, many of whom have shown kindnesses beyond the capabilities of my former all-consuming social circle.

As for myself, I have been up and down, but remain optimistic. Writing my story has brought up a number of suppressed and unprocessed memories. These have taken a toll on me as I have been writing, but it's the start of the healing process. My life is much better now, and I no longer have the same internal conflicts that were present before. My dearest Imogen has stood by me through some very difficult times indeed. She has seen the damage caused as I have tried to break the mental programming. She has rejoiced in the progress I have made and cried at the setbacks I have suffered. Without her I know not where I would be. This too applies to my dear friend Jake, who has battled alongside me in search of peace. Peace of mind in light of a broken dream, a shattered former reality.

Am I free from emotional damage? Not at all. There are many issues that continue to plague my waking existence, but there is still hope for me, as there is for any others who are having doubts. Doubts about a religion that claims ultimate truth, demands so much of its followers, yet disallows questioning and criticism in any form.

It is my hope that the following chapters help all who read them to see *the truth* behind 'the truth'.

CHAPTER 5

THE HISTORY LESSON

1799 - PRESENT

The Watchtower Society, the main corporation behind the Jehovah's Witnesses, is a multinational organisation. In 2001 it was reported to have an annual income of over $950 million. It was listed in the top forty of New York's highest earning corporations. Due to the fact that volunteers perform most, if not all work, they have minimal expenses other than the printing and distribution costs of their religious magazines, books, and leaflets. Their total assets are likely to be worth in the region of several billion dollars. As with most religious groups, they enjoy tax relief status and even get many benefits like the 'Gift Aid' arrangement in the United Kingdom. Clearly it is a wealthy organisation, but it, like most others had to start somewhere. As I learned more and more about the history of the religion, I become both shocked and disillusioned. A summary of my findings is presented in this chapter.

Much (if not all) of the history of Jehovah's Witnesses that is known to followers of the religion is learned from the Watchtower publication 'Jehovah's Witnesses – Proclaimers of God's Kingdom'. Much of the disturbing *true* history of the Watchtower Society has been either left out entirely or heavily 'sugar coated'; however, there still are notable instances of questionable actions, beliefs and teachings, all of which serve as testimony against the claim that they are in fact God's chosen organisation.

Charles Taze Russell

This highly respected founder of the Watchtower Bible and Tract Society started his spiritual quest in the 1870s. The Adventist movement and recent friendship with Nelson Barbour, a publisher of the religious magazine 'Herald of the Morning' heavily influenced him. Barbour's fixation with chronology and biblical prophecy captivated the interest and focus of Russell, who sold his father's prosperous clothing chain for the then small fortune of $300,000 to further this work. Russell's cash injection aided the publication

Charles Taze Russell

of literature that claimed the Bible foretold the resurrection of all dead Christians in 1878. When this failed to materialise, Russell and Barbour began to dispute the reasons for their error, which ultimately led to their separation, and ended their friendship.

Having retained much of his fortune, Russell started his own religious journal entitled 'Zion's Watch Tower and Herald of Christ's Presence' in 1879, followed by the formation of 'Zion's Watch Tower Tract Society' in 1881. He quickly gained recognition and was able to print and distribute his literature to a large and growing audience by the use of his own funds and donations from followers. Russell had developed an obsession with prophetic dates and publicised his expectations which were lapped-up by his followers. His key chronological doctrine was that the 'last days' began in 1799, Jesus Christ began ruling in heaven in 1879, and the 'end of the time of trouble' (i.e. paradise conditions) would commence in 1914. The following quote is from a section entitled, 'Can it be delayed until 1914?'

> "We see no reason for changing the figures – nor could we change them if we would. They are, we believe, God's dates, not ours. But bear in mind the end of 1914 is not the date for the beginning, but for the end of the time of trouble." – *Zion's Watch Tower*, July 15th 1894, p.226.

There was much hype generated in the date 1914 and the start of World War I only cemented the faith of the followers, even when Armageddon didn't arrive. The Watch Tower Society however was quick to cover the error up as the following quotes show.

Studies in the Scriptures Series III - Thy Kingdom Come 1908 Edition:

> "That the deliverance of the saints **must take place some time before 1914** is manifest, since the deliverance of fleshly Israel, as we shall see, is appointed to take place at that time, and the angry nations will then be authoritatively commanded to be still, and will be made to recognize the power of Jehovah's Anointed. **Just how long before 1914** the last living members of the body of Christ will be glorified, we are not directly informed..."

Studies in the Scriptures Series III - Thy Kingdom Come 1915 Edition:

> "That the deliverance of the saints **must take place very soon after 1914** is manifest, since the deliverance of fleshly Israel, as we shall see, is appointed to take place at that time, and the angry nations will then be authoritatively commanded to be still, and will be made to recognize the power of Jehovah's Anointed. **Just how

long after 1914 the last living members of the body of Christ will be glorified, we are not directly informed..."

This questionable tactic seems to have been employed many times throughout the organisation's history, and has served it well as I will later demonstrate. For now though, we will look at one of Charles Taze Russell's most bizarre teachings.

Pyramidology

Russell developed a fascination with the Great Pyramid of Giza. Following the work of Charles Smyth, Joseph Seiss and others, he determined that this pyramid was 'God's Stone Witness' and the measurements of the internal passageways confirmed biblical prophecy.

> "Prof. Smyth found the first of these measures (a) to be 1874 Pyramid inches, the second (b), 1881 Pyramid inches, and the third (c), 1910 Pyramid inches; Thus reduced, they would give the dates (a) October, 1874, (b) October, 1881 and (c) October, 1910 A.D." - *Thy Kingdom Come*, p.362.

The main teachings regarding the Great Pyramid were explained in the Studies in the Scriptures Series. One such volume was entitled 'The Divine Plan of the Ages – As Shown in the Great Pyramid'. Russell wrote it in 1886. Inside the pages of this book Russell describes the metaphorical significance and similarities of the great pyramid.

> "Our oneness with the Lord Jesus, as members of the Christ, the anointed company, is well illustrated by the figure of the pyramid. The top-stone is a perfect pyramid of itself. Other stones may be built up under it, and, if in harmony with all the characteristic lines of the top-stone, the whole mass will be a perfect pyramid. How beautifully this illustrates our position as members of "the Seed"-- "the Christ." – *The Divine Plan of the Ages,* p.82.

The book goes into detail as to the meaning of the capstone, the significance of the various levels and all manner of points relating to the exterior of the construct.

> "Adam was a perfect being, pyramid a. Notice its position--on plane N, which represents human perfection. On plane R, the plane of sin and imperfection or the depraved plane, the topless pyramid, b, an imperfect figure, represents fallen Adam and his posterity--depraved, sinful and condemned." – *The Divine Plan of the Ages*, p.228.

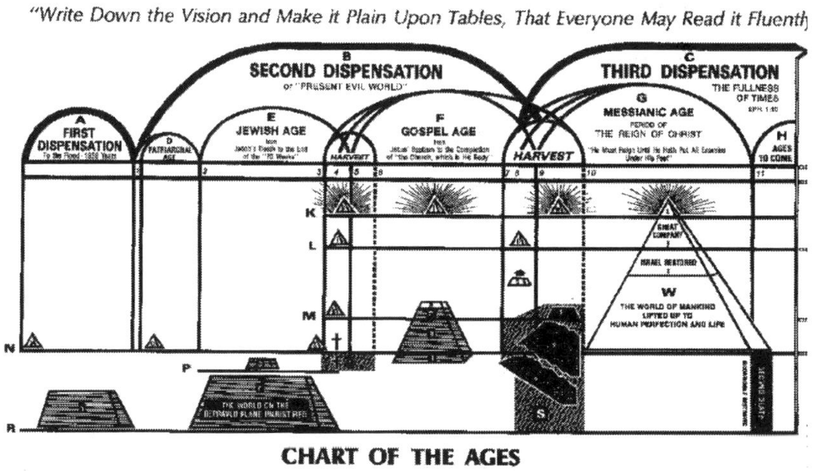

Figure 1: Chart of the Ages Foldout

The front of the book contains a foldout illustration that explains the parallels between the Great Pyramid and God's plan. (Figure 1)

This pyramid teaching was not a mere illustration to help the followers understand biblical points. It was a doctrinal core belief that appears to be as important as the Bible itself to the founders and followers of the time.

Upon the realisation that 1874 might not have been quite right as the start of 'the time of trouble', Russell had to make some adjustments to buy more time. In 1910 he changed the measurements of some of the internal passageways that were used to calculate / verify biblical prophecy.

Thy Kingdom Come p.342 <u>1891 Edition:</u>

> "Then measuring down the "Entrance Passage" from that point, to find the distance to the entrance of the "Pit," representing the great trouble and destruction with which this age is to close, when evil will be overthrown from power, we find it to be **3416 inches, symbolizing 3416 years from the above date, BC 1542. This calculation shows AD. 1874 as marking the beginning of the period of trouble; for 1542 years BC plus 1874 years AD. equals 3416 years. Thus the Pyramid witnesses that the close of 1874** was the chronological beginning of the time of trouble such as was not since there was a nation -- no, nor ever shall be afterward. And thus it will be noted that this "Witness" <u>fully corroborates the Bible testimony on this subject</u>..."

Thy Kingdom Come p.342 <u>1910 Edition:</u>

> "Then measuring down the "Entrance Passage" from that point, to find the distance to the entrance of the "Pit," representing the great trouble and destruction with which this age is to close, when evil will be overthrown from power, we find it to be **3457 inches, symbolizing 3457 years from the above date, BC 1542. This calculation shows AD. 1915 as marking the beginning of the period of trouble; for 1542 years BC plus 1915 years AD. equals 3457 years. Thus the Pyramid witnesses that the close of 1914** will be the beginning of the time of trouble such as was not since there was a nation -- no, nor ever shall be afterward. And thus it will be

noted that this "Witness" <u>fully corroborates</u> the' Bible testimony on this subject..."

(See Appendix 'A' for the scans of the above quotes).

Russell's Memorial Stone

Charles T Russell died in 1916 having not seen the promised new order. A few yards from his grave, the Watchtower Society installed a large stone pyramid as a memorial stone dedicated to Russell and other faithful followers who had passed away. The monument features the engraved words 'Watchtower Bible and Tract Society' as well as 'Risen with Christ'. An open book is carved on one side with 'C T Russell' as the first entry. This book would logically resemble the 'book of life' as described in Revelation, the final book of the Bible. A masonic 'Cross & Crown' symbol within a wreath is also present.

Russell's Memorial Stone

(See Appendix 'B' for the original drawing of the monument).

The memorial stone and Russell's actual grave lay within a stone's throw of the Greater Pittsburgh Masonic Centre. Whether Russell secretly was a Freemason remains to be established. However there are several who believe he was, and Russell himself admitted some association with them.

"You know our order is so secret we cannot know each other always. Is not that wonderful? I find that is so with Masons also.

Many Masons shake hands with me and give me what I know is their grip; they don't know me from a Mason. Something I do seems to be the same as Masons do, I don't know what it is; but they often give me all kinds of grips and I give them back, then I tell them I don't know anything about it except just a few grips that have come to me naturally." - *Pastor Russell's Convention Discourses*.

The teachings related to pyramids continued under the leadership of Judge Rutherford for years after Russell's death, and long after Jesus Christ's apparent inspection of the world's religions in 1919.

"In the great Pyramid of Egypt, standing as a silent and inanimate witness of the Lord, is a messenger; and its testimony speaks with great eloquence concerning the divine plan." - *The Watchtower*, May 15th 1925, p.148.

The years 1914 and 1918/19 would remain crucial dates in Watchtower chronology, having World War I as apparent proof of their significance.

Judge Joseph Rutherford

Upon the death of Russell, there was need of new leadership. Joseph F Rutherford, a Missouri lawyer who had served as the Watchtower Society's legal counsel, saw to it that he would take charge. Using legal and apparently less than Christ-like tactics, Rutherford ensured he remained in charge of the Society after he was elected in 1917. A mere five months after his election, four of the board of directors decided they had made an error of judgement when voting for Rutherford as president. They feared that Rutherford's position had become autocratic. Action was taken to reclaim authority from the president and return it to the board. Rutherford claimed this was a mutiny, and had his opposers removed and later replaced.

Having acted as a stand-in judge on occasion, the new leader of the Watchtower Society adopted the name Judge Rutherford. By 1919 approximately one out of every seven Bible Students had left the organisation because of Rutherford's teachings and rules. Among the many doctrinal changes he initiated was the teaching that Christ invisibly returned in 1914, instead of 1878 as was previously taught. For a time the battle of Armageddon was taught to be 1918. This clearly failed to occur and Rutherford and seven of the board of directors were imprisoned in 1918 for promoting the refusal of military service. The main evidence used against them was the recently published title 'The Finished Mystery', which described patriotism as murder amongst other things.

Judge Joseph Rutherford

> "Nowhere in the New Testament is Patriotism (a narrow-minded hatred of other peoples) encouraged." – *The Finished Mystery*, p.247.

The imprisoned leaders were released in 1919 and all charges were eventually dropped. In 1920 Rutherford started the 'Millions Campaign'. A new booklet was released entitled 'Millions Now Living Will Never Die". Several doctrinal changes were outlined in this publication. One of which was that God would start to resurrect ancient faithful servants including Abraham, Isaac, and Noah in 1925. Despite no such death reversals, Rutherford stuck to the story and, in 1929 solicited funds to construct a ten-bedroom mansion in San Diego. This 'palace' was deeded to the faithful patriarchs that had still not arrived. The glorious home was given the name 'Beth Sarim' (House of Princes). Rutherford conveniently volunteered to be the home's 'caretaker' whilst the wait for the promised resurrection took place.

Whilst much of the world and indeed the Brothers and Sisters endured bitter suffering at the hands of 'The Great Depression', Rutherford lived in luxurious comfort. It was reported by several that he frequently requested crates of various liquors delivered to the house primarily for his consumption. While some at Watchtower headquarters viewed him as 'charitable and generous' others claimed he was '*blunt and moody with an explosive temper*', and a '*dogmatic and insensitive person, obsessed with his own self-importance*'. In addition to the mansion, Rutherford had the use of at least one 16 cylinder Cadillac automobile, perhaps further adding insult to injury to his deprived followers. It was under Rutherford's leadership that the movement adopted the name 'Jehovah's Witnesses'. Rutherford died in 1942 at Beth Sarim aged 72. The Watchtower Society sold the home in 1948 making a statement that it had '*fully served its purpose...*' (This couldn't be further from the truth).

Beth Sarim - House of the Princes

Questionable Symbols

During these early years, the use of symbols in the magazines, on the memorial pyramid and in books was extensive.

> "For years, Bible Students wore a cross and crown as a badge of identification, and this symbol was on the front cover of the "Watch Tower" from 1891 to 1931." - *Jehovah's Witnesses - Proclaimers of God's Kingdom*, p.200.

The 'Cross & Crown' is a symbol used by Freemasons (as mentioned earlier). An Egyptian 'Winged Sun Disc' also featured on the front of other publications such as *The Finished Mystery*. Such pagan symbols

The Watchtower Featuring Cross & Crown Symbol

(that apparently are disgusting to God) saw heavy use in these early days. Yet the religion was still heralded 'The Truth' by its followers.

Johannes Greber

Mr Greber had previously been a member of the Catholic Clergy but had left to pursue his own religious endeavours. The Watchtower Society publicly denounced him as early as 1955 for engaging in Spiritistic practices.

> "It comes as no surprise that the one Johannes Greber, a former Catholic clergyman, has become a spiritualist and has published the book entitled 'Communication with the Spirit World: Its Laws and Its Purpose.'" - *The Watchtower,* Oct 1st 1955, p.603.

The Society however later used Greber's Bible translation in support of its own. It was subsequently claimed that Greber only revealed his occult connections in a later edition of his work.

> "This translation was used occasionally in support of renderings of Matthew 27:52, 53 and John 1:1, as given in the *New World Translation* and other authoritative Bible versions. But as indicated in a foreword to the 1980 edition of *The New Testament* by Johannes

Greber, this translator relied on "God's Spirit World" to clarify for him how he should translate difficult passages. It is stated: "His wife, a medium of God's Spiritworld was often instrumental in conveying the correct answers from God's Messengers to Pastor Greber." *The Watchtower* has deemed it improper to make use of a translation that has such a close rapport with spiritism." - *The Watchtower, Apr 1st 1983, p.31.*

The Watchtower Society prides itself on a commitment to honesty and spiritual cleanliness, yet here we find conflicting statements. It's a troubling discovery, since Jehovah's Witnesses trust the information provided by their leadership implicitly.

Vaccines

The Watchtower Society even prohibited vaccinations. They were condemned as wicked an evil.

> "Vaccination never prevented anything and never will, and is the most barbarous practice...We are in the last days; and the devil is slowly losing his hold, making a strenuous effort meanwhile to do all the damage he can, and to his credit can such evils be placed...Use your rights as American citizens to forever abolish the devilish practice of vaccinations." - *Golden Age (later renamed Awake!), Oct 12th 1921, p.17.*

Much later on however, the opposite viewpoint was published. Furthermore a distortion is made of their previous statements that condemned vaccines.

> "Previous articles in this journal and its companion, The Watchtower, have presented a consistent position: It would be up to the Bible-trained conscience of the individual Christian as to whether he would accept [vaccinations] for himself and his family." - *Awake!* Aug 8th 1993, p.25.

Not only is this misleading, it overlooks those who may well have lost their lives by following the incorrect previous teaching, that apparently came from God at the time, yet was eventually changed.

Organ Transplants

Initially, organ transplants were considered a personal decision. This was later changed when such treatments were deemed by the Society as abhorrent.

> "...sustaining one's life by means of the body or part of the body of another human...would be cannibalism..." - *The Watchtower,* Nov 15th 1967, p.702.

This was later changed back to the original teaching.

> "There is no Biblical command pointedly forbidding the taking in of other human tissue. It is a matter for personal decision." - *The Watchtower,* Mar 15th 1980, p.31.

Throughout the many years the ban on organ transplants was in force, how many people died as a result of this false doctrine? All the while it was being hailed as 'The Truth'. The Watchtower Society has made no apology for the previous false teachings that no doubt ended the lives of their faithful followers. These ones died trusting in the 'Faithful Slave' only for the rule to be reversed a mere few years later.

Other Medical Advice

In it's infancy the Watchtower Society printed some truly bizarre medical advice. Two of the worst offenders were:

> "If any overzealous doctor condemns your tonsils go and commit suicide with a case-knife. It's cheaper and less painful." - *Golden Age*, Apr 7th 1926, p.438.

"Sleep on the right side or flat on your back, with the head toward the north so as to get benefit of the earth's magnetic currents. Avoid serum inoculations as they pollute the blood stream with their filthy pus.... Stop chewing gum, as you need the saliva for your food." - *Golden Age,* Nov 12th 1929, p.107.

Any non-Witnesses reading this may not be surprised and conclude these are simply the ramblings of yet another kooky religion. To a Witness however, such revelations of purely ludicrous statements come as a shock. The organisation is supposed to be directed by God's spirit, yet when such oddities are discovered a sense of disbelief is present. This is hardly surprising since Witnesses firmly believe they are follower the only true religion.

The New World Translation - Translators

The Jehovah's Witness Bible has received praise as well as criticism. However, the Watchtower Society has repeatedly caused upset by quoting many notable scholars out of context. On many occasions they have misquoted individuals in a manner that shows support for their New World Translation. In fact the opposite was often the case. Scholar Dr Julius Mantey was one such individual and he wrote to the Watchtower Society showing "...examples of Watchtower mistranslations and perversions of God's Word.". He went on to write: "because you have been quoting me out of context, I herewith request you not to quote the *Manual Grammar of the Greek New Testament* again, which you have been doing for 24 years.". (Full letter available in Appendix 'C' which outlines examples of how Dr Mantey felt his work was abused).

In addition to general criticism targeting those passages shown to contain biases towards Watchtower doctrines, the original translators themselves have come under scrutiny. The names and qualifications of the creators of the New World Translation remained unknown for years.

They were not published for the claimed reason of humility. Raymond Franz was the nephew of the president of the Watchtower Society Fred Franz. He served as a member of the Governing Body for nine of his sixty years serving as a Jehovah's Witness. After being conspired against and removed from office and later the religion entirely, he wrote and published one of the best exposés ever produced on Jehovah's Witnesses. The book 'Crisis Of Conscience' (1983) explains that of the four men who made up the translation team, only his uncle Fred Franz had any training in Greek. He had studied it for two years and was only self-taught in Hebrew. Interestingly in a court case, Fred Franz was asked to translate a simple passage from the Bible (Genesis 2:4). He refused stating, "No I wouldn't attempt to do that". Quite how this clearly incompetent team managed to translate the whole Bible, remains to be explained.

Malawi – Mexico Scandal

One of the more upsetting revelations in 'Crisis Of Conscience' is the scandal involving Brothers and Sisters in both Malawi and Mexico. In 1964 the Witnesses in Malawi began suffering beatings, abuse, rape, and murder. The reason for this was the order from the Governing Body that Witnesses were not allowed to purchase a political card stating their citizenship and submission to the party in power at the time. Malawi is a one party state and the president is in power for life. There were no competing parties to choose from, nor any politics to get involved with. The view from the Society was that to purchase this card would be a violation of the neutrality that is required of all Witnesses. Any Witness reading this so far would unhesitatingly be in agreement, despite the disturbing consequences. Where it becomes sickening is the fact that the opposite standard was upheld in Mexico at the same time.

Males in Mexico were required to complete one year of military training. Upon completion, they were awarded a 'Cartilla' that certified their training and meant that the individual was now in the first reserve of the army. Witnesses view involvement with the military as at least as serious (if not more so) than such in politics. Yet the position of the Governing Body was far less strict. The official policy was that Brothers were permitted (if their conscience allowed) to pay a bribe to the officer in charge. The bribe would get them the 'Cartilla' but they would not have to complete the training. However, the individual was still a member of the army reserve and should they be called to war, they would be on their own, so to speak. When the Brothers in Mexico heard how their fellow followers were suffering in Malawi, they were conscience-stricken. This double standard was not well known far outside these countries, until the publication of 'Crisis of Conscience'.

1975

Despite the 'playing down' of the facts in later Watchtower literature, 1975 was heavily influential in growing the religion's follower base, and significant financial gains were made. A plethora of talks, magazines, and books built the expectations of the Brothers and Sisters that 1975 would almost certainly be the arrival of Armageddon.

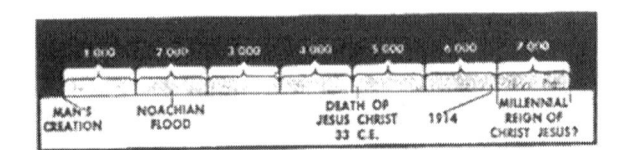

Time Chart Indicating Armageddon Would Occur in 1975

..Jehovah has provided meat in due season. Because he's held up before all of us, a new goal. A new year. Something to reach out for and it just seems it has given all of us so much more energy and power in this final burst of speed to the finish line. And that's the year 1975. Well, **we don't have to guess what the year 1975 means if we read the Watchtower. And don't wait 'till 1975. The door is going to be shut before then**. As one brother put it, "Stay alive to Seventy-Five"" - *1967 District Convention, Wisconsin.*

"The immediate future is certain to be filled with climactic events, for this old system is nearing its complete end. **Within a few years at most** the final parts of Bible prophecy relative to these "last days" will undergo fulfilment." - *The Watchtower*, May 1st 1968.

"The fact that fifty-four years of the period called the "last days" have already gone by is highly significant. It means that **only a few years, at most**, remain before the corrupt system of things dominating the earth is destroyed by God." - *Awake!* Oct 8th 1968, p.13-14.

"If you are a young person, you also need to face the fact that **you will never grow old in this present system of things**. Why not? Because all the evidence in fulfillment of Bible prophecy indicates that **this corrupt system is due to end in a few years. Of the generation that observed the beginning of the "last days" in 1914, Jesus foretold: "This generation will by no means pass away until all these things occur."**-Matt. 24:34. Therefore, as a young person, you will never fulfill any career that this system offers. If you are in highschool and thinking about a college education, it means at least four, perhaps even six or eight more years to graduate into a specialized career. **But where will this system of things be by that time? It will be well on the way toward its finish, if not actually gone!**" - *Awake! May 22nd 1969, p.15.*

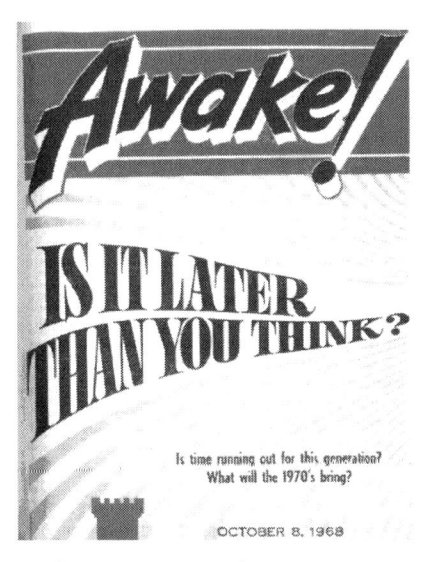

Awake! Magazine Built Expectation Too

"Another speaker, F. W. Franz, the Society's vice-president, forcefully impressed on the audience the urgency of the Christian preaching work. He stressed that, **according to dependable Bible chronology, 6,000 years of human history will end this coming**

One of Many Articles Highlighting the Significance of 1975

September according to the lunar calendar. This coincides with a time when "the human species [is] about to starve itself to death," as well as its being faced with poisoning by pollution and destruction by nuclear weapons. Franz added: **"There's no basis for believing that mankind, faced with what it now faces, can exist for the seventh thousand-year period"** under the present system

JW Convention Attendee Name Badge

of things. Does this mean that we know exactly when God will destroy this old system and establish a new one? Franz showed that we do not, for we do not know how short was the time interval between Adam's creation and the creation of Eve, at which point God's rest day of seven thousand years began. (Heb. 4:3, 4) But, he pointed out, **"we should not think that this year of 1975 is of no significance** to us," for the Bible proves that Jehovah is "the greatest chronologist" and **"we have the anchor date, 1914,** marking the end of the Gentile Times." So, he continued, **"we are filled with anticipation for the near future, for our generation."** — Matt. 24:34." - *The Watchtower,* May 1st 1975, p.285.

"And now, as the year 1975 opens up, some thousands of the anointed remnant, still alive on this earth, look ahead to realizing that joyful prospect. The increasing "great crowd" of their sheeplike companions look forward with them to entering the New Order without interruption of life." - *The Watchtower,* Dec 15th 1974, p.766.

In addition to the anticipation of what 1975 would bring, the Watchtower Society printed articles that praised Witnesses who sold their homes to fund full-time preaching work. Many of whom also donated large proceeds to the Society.

"Reports are heard of **brothers selling their homes and property and planning to finish out the rest of their days in this old system in the pioneer service.** Certainly this is a fine way to spend the short time remaining before the wicked world's end." - *Kingdom Ministry,* May 1974, p.3.

According to Raymond Franz, in and around 1975 the Watchtower Society had property, stocks, bonds, and shares worth in excess of $300,000,000. The Watchtower Society wasn't selling in 1975, it was buying, and at an increased rate.

When 1975 failed to produce the expected results, the Watchtower Society changed some of its publications to hide the error.

"Back in 1960, a former United States Secretary of State, Dean Acherson declared that our time is "a period of unequaled instability, unequaled violence" And he warned: "I know enough of what is going on to assure you that, **in fifteen years from today** this world is going to be too dangerous to live in"" - *The Truth That Leads to Eternal Life,* p.9, 1968 edition.

The crucial part of this statement was changed in the 1981 edition.

"Also, as reported back in 1960, a former United States Secretary of State, Dean Acheson, declared that our time is "a period of unequaled instability, unequaled violence." Based on what he knew was then going on in the world, it was his conclusion that **soon** "this world is going to be too dangerous to live in."" - *The Truth That Leads to Eternal Life,* p.9, 1981 edition.

The Watchtower Society had previously put the blame for the error solely on the Brothers and Sisters for 'reading into things' too much. The Watchtower July 15th 1976 explains:

"It may be that some who have been serving God have planned their lives according to a mistaken view of just what was to happen on a certain date or in a certain year. They may have, for this reason, put off or neglected things that they otherwise would have cared for. But they have missed the point of the Bible's warnings concerning the end of this system of things, thinking that Bible chronology reveals the specific date."

The article continues to drum the point home:

"But it is not advisable for us to set our sights on a certain date, neglecting everyday things we would ordinarily care for as Christians, such as things that we and our families really need. We may be forgetting that, when the "day" comes, it will not change the principle that Christians must at all times take care of all their responsibilities. If anyone has been disappointed through not following this line of thought, he should now concentrate on adjusting his viewpoint, seeing that it was not the word of God that failed or deceived him and brought disappointment, but that his own understanding was based on wrong premises."

These and other statements were hardly the apology that the Brothers and Sisters deserved. Only later was anything like an admission of error made.

> "With the appearance of the book *Life Everlasting-in Freedom of the Sons of God*, and its comments as to how appropriate it would be for the millennial reign of Christ to parallel the seventh millennium of man's existence, **considerable expectation was aroused regarding the year 1975**. There were statements made then, and thereafter, stressing that this was only a possibility. Unfortunately, however, along with such cautionary information, **there were other statements published that implied that such realization of hopes by that year was more of a probability than a mere possibility.** It is to be regretted that **these latter statements apparently overshadowed the cautionary ones** and contributed to a buildup of the expectation already initiated." - *The Watchtower*, Mar 15th 1980, p.17.

Nevertheless, many Witnesses left the religion after 1975 as a result of the let-down and lack of apology from the Governing Body. These ones would be subjected to shunning by their Witness friends and family.

United Nations Association

In October 2001, the Guardian newspaper printed an article exposing Jehovah's Witnesses for being linked to the United Nations, despite denouncing it at the same time. The article was entitled 'Jehovah's Witnesses link to UN queried', and created quite a stir. It was revealed that the Watchtower Society had been discretely registered as a member of the United Nations Department of Public Information (UNDPI) in 1992. Knowing their strict rules on political neutrality, the Watchtower Society acted swiftly in requesting to be disaffiliated from the UN once the story went public. A defence was made by the Society that they only registered with the UNDPI in order to use the library facilities. Due to the large numbers of enquiries made, the UN released the following statement.

(See Appendix 'D' for a full scan of the letter).

The letter even states that by accepting association with the UN, they agree to support its charter. Furthermore, a letter from a UN library even stated that, 'the issuance of a library pass is independent of NGO status or any other status.' and that, 'There has been no change in the library pass policy in general.' A further statement from the UN stated that, 'The criteria for association for NGOs has not changed since 1991.' All of which goes against what the Society said took place.

Why is this a big deal? The answer is simple: The Watchtower Society maintains a strict stand of political neutrality and demands absolute adherence from its followers. Even the most basic association with an 'unclean' organisation is unacceptable. How does the Watchtower Society view the United Nations?

> "The United Nations is actually a worldly confederacy against Jehovah God and his dedicated Witnesses on earth." - *The Watchtower*, Sep 1st 1987, p.20.

> "No, the UN is not a blessing, even though the religious clergy of Christendom and the rabbis of Jewry pray heaven's blessing upon that organization. It is really "the image of the wild beast," the visible political, commercial organization of "the god of this system of things," Satan the Devil. So the UN will soon be destroyed along with that beastly organization." - *The Watchtower*, Sep 15th 1984, p.15.

> "The UN is actually a blasphemous counterfeit of God's Messianic Kingdom..." - *Revelation Its Grand Climax At Hand!* p.248.

It's clear that the United Nations is disgusting as far as the Watchtower Society is concerned. Why then would it trust the information in their libraries, if that were indeed the reason why they joined in the first place? Furthermore what does the Watchtower Society print regarding membership with other organisations that it regards as 'unclean'?

> "We have long recognized that the YMCA, though not being a church as such, is definitely aligned with the religious organizations of Christendom in efforts to promote interfaith."

The above statement is from a 'Questions From Readers' article in *The Watchtower* Jan 1st 1979 (p.30.). The article continues to explain the significance of membership with any such organisation.

> "In joining the YMCA as a member a person accepts or endorses the general objectives and principles of the organization. ... Membership means that one has become an integral part of this organization founded with definite religious objectives, including the promotion of interfaith. Hence, for one of Jehovah's Witnesses to become a member of such a so-called Christian association would amount to apostasy."

Witnesses are not permitted to join the YMCA for any reason whatsoever. Even if it were to use recreational facilities, it would still be a violation, and therefore be entirely unacceptable. Why then was it permissible for the Society to have any such ties with the UN?

History, Why Does It Matter?

Watchtower Society literature has all too often spurred criticism of other religions. Much of the denigration relates to the pagan origins and practices that preceded the modern interpretations. By its own printed standard however, the Watchtower Society disqualifies itself from the position of the one true religion.

"Do origins really matter? Yes! To illustrate: Suppose you saw a piece of candy lying in the gutter. Would you pick up that candy and eat it? Of course not! That candy is unclean. Like that candy, holidays may seem sweet, but they have been picked up from unclean places. To take a stand for true worship, we need to have a viewpoint like that of the prophet Isaiah, who told true worshipers: "Touch nothing unclean." - *What Does The Bible Really Teach?* p.159.

The history of the Jehovah's Witnesses is replete with errors and false teachings. The use of Egyptian Pyramidology, Pagan and Masonic symbols, false predictions, altered literature, and the rest, all point as evidence that this religion is as poorly founded as the ones it criticises. In addition, the teaching is that Jesus Christ inspected all the world's religions in 1919 and chose the Watchtower Society to 'look after all his belongings'. When the teachings of that time are examined, it is obvious that there is little chance Christ would select this organisation. For more information read 'Captives of a Concept' (2006) by Don Cameron.

After reading some of the frankly ludicrous things that have been taught and published by the Society, one must wonder how anyone can conclude that God was ever directing this organisation.

CHAPTER 6

THE DARK SIDE

A CULT FOLLOWING

Where the line is drawn between an inoffensive moderate religion and something more sinister, is the methodology and motives of those in power. The degree of control held over the ordinary members is also a factor. Are Jehovah's Witnesses part of a cult? There are several meanings to the word 'cult', one of which is so broad that all religions qualify. When most people think of a cult, they envisage high control of its members and secretive and possibly dangerous practices. The World English Dictionary defines 'cult' as the following:

> "A quasi-religious organization using devious psychological techniques to gain and control adherents"

This is one of the more extreme definitions, but we will see how the Jehovah's Witness religion fairs when held up against it.

A Cult?

America's leading exit-counsellor[1] Steven Hassan has written several notable books on the subject of cults. One such publication is Combatting Cult Mind Control[2]. As I read through this excellent resource, I noticed how nearly every instance it describes how cults operate paralleled almost exactly with what I have seen within the Jehovah's Witnesses. It is my intention to avail the reader with some examples that really show the religion for what it is. The book is replete with such examples, however I will share those that struck me the most and explain how they apply in the case of Jehovah's Witnesses.

> "Even though most cult members tell you they are "happier than they've ever been in their lives," the reality is sadly different." - *Combating Cult Mind Control,* Park Street Press, 1990. p.50.

This is so very true as Witnesses are taught that they are in a 'Spiritual Paradise' and are God's 'Happy People'. Though they face the pressures of 'The World' and are fighting to keep to God's 'righteous standards', they are happy because they have *The Truth*. In addition they believe that they are part of the only religion that is united in true worship, and the only group that will survive God's judgement day. This gives them the feeling of group strength and solidarity. However, many Witnesses suffer from depression and are in fact far from happy.

Though this next quote is describing how children are educated, it is equally true how ALL Witnesses perceive things within the walls of the Watchtower.

---

[1] An Exit-Counsellor is a professional who helps individuals mentally free themselves from high-control groups.
[2] Published by Park Street Press, 1990.

> "...they are taught that the world is a hostile, evil place, and are forced to depend on cult doctrine to understand reality." - *Combating Cult Mind Control,* Park Street Press, 1990. p.51.

I don't think I need to explain this one as I feel it is clear from previous chapters that it is true. The world is indeed viewed as a wicked place filled with nasty, selfish, unloving people who are under Satan's control. This kind of thinking becomes deeply embedded and takes people years to adjust to more realistic and moderate views after escaping the religion.

B.I.T.E Model for Cults

Steve Hassan created the B.I.T.E model, which outlines the criteria for cults. BITE is broken down into the following four key sections of control: Behavioural Control, Information Control, Thought Control and Emotional Control. We will analyse each of these here in relation to the Jehovah's Witness religion.

Behavioural Control

> [3] *"Where, how and with whom the member lives and associates with."*

While Witnesses are not segregated physically from the rest of the world, they are to remain separate spiritually. Unnecessary association with 'worldly' people is very much frowned upon, and can even lead to an individual being 'marked' themselves as bad association. Former members must be shunned and treated as though they do not even exist.

> *"What clothes, colors, hairstyles the person wears"*

---

[3] The following italicised quotes in this chapter are from Steve Hassan's website http://www.freedomofmind.com/Info/BITE/bitemodel.php where he outlines the B.I.T.E Model for Cults.

Dress and grooming is closely monitored and loving council is given where individuals fail to adhere to the requirements. In Western countries, Brothers must wear suits and ties when at congregation meetings or when engaging in the door-to-door preaching work. Men's hair should be short and tidy. Facial hair is not permitted (except eyebrows). Sisters are to wear dresses (trousers are not permitted). Skirts must not be higher than the knee. Some jewellery and makeup is allowed, but modesty is keenly highlighted.[4]

> *"Major time commitment required for indoctrination sessions and group rituals"*

Witnesses are expected to attend every meeting each week, which at the time of writing is two on a Sunday and two on a weekday. They are to pre-study for these meetings so as to be able to participate in the question and answer segments. Personal Bible reading and Personal Study (research into Bible topics that interest the individual) are expected as well as family study time. Brothers are often given talks to prepare to deliver from the platform at the mid-week meeting, which requires planning, practice and preparation. The door-to-door work is extremely important and individuals are set a goal of at least 10 hours per month in this work. Naturally, additional time is required to suitably prepare for each outing.

> *"Individualism discouraged; group think prevails"*

I have previously discussed the Watchtower's strong council to avoid 'Independent Thinking'. As long as one agrees with and follows the teachings of the Watchtower Society, a Witness is free to enjoy the association and love of the congregation. Congregation meetings are replete with comments of praise for God and his 'chosen organisation'.

---

[4] Note that these regulations are not all necessarily bad, but it is the level of control that is exercised that is the issue.

Critical comments are never uttered, and any who dared to would be quickly 'marked' as weak, or even Apostate.

> *"Need for obedience and dependency"*

Obedience to 'Jehovah's Commandments' is expected of all Witnesses. A Witness who wants to please God must earnestly strive to be loyal and faithful in all aspects of his or her life, from the very smallest of things to the very largest. Witnesses must also rely solely on the Watchtower Society to provide them with 'spiritual food' to guide them in their lives. No one can gain a full understanding of the Bible or gain God's full approval without obedience to the Watchtower Society

Information Control

> *"Use of deception*
>
> *a. Deliberately holding back information*
>
> *b. Distorting information to make it acceptable*
>
> *c. Outright lying"*

As you will have noticed, the Watchtower Society seems quite happy to provide its followers with biased and inaccurate information.

> "While malicious lying is definitely condemned in the Bible, this does not mean that a person is under obligation to divulge truthful information to people who are not entitled to it." – *Insight on the Scriptures: Volume 2*, 1988, p.244-245.

One surely has to wonder how many subjects are falsely portrayed to regular Witnesses, and in turn the householders who give them an ear.

> *"Access to non-cult sources of information minimized or discouraged*

a. Books, articles, newspapers, magazines, TV, radio

b. Critical information

c. Former members

d. Keep members so busy they don't have time to think"

Secular sources may be used to back up the claims and teachings of the Watchtower, but they can never be viewed as reliable. After all, they are the work of imperfect and fallible men. Anything that is critical of the Watchtower Society or the teachings of Jehovah's Witnesses is to be avoided, especially that of former members (Apostates).

> "In Jehovah's organization it is not necessary to spend a lot of time and energy in research, for there are brothers in the organization who are assigned to that very thing..." - *The Watchtower*, Jun 1st 1967, p.338.

In addition to being actively discouraged from doing extensive independent research, the massive amount of time spent engaging in Watchtower activities means Witnesses have little time or energy left over.

"Extensive use of cult generated information and propaganda

a. Newsletters, magazines, journals, audio tapes, videotapes, etc.

b. Misquotations, statements taken out of context from non-cult sources" [5]

The sheer volume of literature that Witnesses are bombarded with from their leadership is somewhat astounding. It is often said that the Brothers

---

[5] Chapter 7 discusses misquotations and out of context statements.

can't keep up with the massive provision of 'Spiritual Food'. Watchtower and Awake! magazines, new books, brochures, tracts, Our Kingdom Ministry journals and even DVDs and audio recordings are ever more fervently being produced.

Thought Control

If you can control how a person or group of people thinks, you can control every aspect of their lives. The B.I.T.E. model breaks down thought control as follows:

> *"Need to internalize the group's doctrine as 'Truth'"*

Almost ironically, a term that is without doubt the most commonly used phrase by Jehovah's Witnesses is 'The Truth'. It is uttered so frequently as a means of referring to the Jehovah's Witness religion, and yet goes unnoticed as (what I propose is) a textbook mind control technique. Some religious cults use similar terms such as *the path, the way,* or *the life*. Jehovah's Witnesses may have the most effective one ever devised.

2013 Worldwide District Convention Public Invitation, entitled 'Truth'

This term *The Truth* is one of the finest examples of 'loaded language' in existence. Frequent use of the phrase instils in the mind of a Witness that what he believes is the absolute truth about life, death, and beyond. If you've never had the experience of hearing this phrase used so often and so casually, you might find it hard to believe that it's even an issue. I must insist you look at the fact that this expression works on the subconscious level of believers and its ready and frequent use 'hard-wires' it onto the mind. As a Witness lives his or her life this acts as a constant reminder that they are in the truth, part of the truth, and working for the truth. This is not only present in the mind; it is persistent, and deeply burrowed. It is for these reasons I call it a textbook mind control or brainwashing technique.

It is an integral reaffirmation of the validity of the Witness belief structure. Calling it The Truth creates a mental block on questioning whether it is actually truth, or just belief. 'The Truth' = Watchtower Society = 'God's Chosen Messenger' = Unquestionable Fact.

> *"Adopt "loaded" language (characterized by "thought-terminating clichés"). Words are the tools we use to think with."*

Loaded language is very much in use by Witnesses. Beyond the already mentioned term *The Truth*, there are many examples of loaded words and phrases that act as 'thought-stoppers'. An example is the powerful word 'Apostate'. To a Witness, hearing this word evokes fear and a 'spiritual guard' would go up. One would flee from anyone who is an Apostate, desperate to avoid hearing anything that might damage their faith. By labelling someone an Apostate, you disarm anything they may say. Witnesses will refuse to listen to them, talk with them, or indeed have anything to do with them. The Witness disregards the labelled person on the basis of the label alone, refusing to judge what they have to say on its own merits.

"Suppose that a doctor told you to avoid contact with someone who is infected with a contagious, deadly disease. You would know what the doctor means, and you would strictly heed his warning. Well, apostates are "mentally diseased," and they seek to infect others with their disloyal teachings... What is involved in avoiding false teachers? We do not receive them into our homes or greet them. We also refuse to read their literature, watch TV programs that feature them, examine their Web sites, or add our comments to their blogs. Why do we take such a firm stand? Because of love. We love "the God of truth," so we are not interested in twisted teachings that contradict his Word of truth." – *The Watchtower*, 15th July 2011, p.15-19.

Would the book you are reading now be considered 'Apostate literature'? Undoubtedly, and very few Witnesses would even pick it up to read the back cover, let alone open it to look inside. Should someone accidentally start reading it, they would quickly hear alarm bells ringing with the word Apostate jumping out at them. A typical Witness would immediately become unsettled and slam the book shut and return it to the shelf. Many would also pray to Jehovah for his Holy Spirit to guard them from any satanic influence they may have been subjected to. I'm not joking either. Such is the power of loaded language when used to trigger fear, guilt and other emotions.

Look back at chapter 1 and see how many terms needed to be explained in detail for a proper understanding of the Jehovah's Witness belief structure to be given. This book only covers the essential terms, but there are many more that I didn't include in the interest of being concise. Another excellent example is the term 'Faithful and Discreet Slave'. This phrase is used to refer to the leadership of the Witnesses and subtly separates the notion that it is a small group of men who dictate the beliefs, rules and regulations for the entire religion. The word 'Faithful' reaffirms that they are loyal and trustworthy, whilst the word 'Discreet' reminds Witnesses that their leaders are humble and don't search for reverence. The word 'Slave' instils the thought that it is the Governing Body that is working for Witnesses, with their tireless efforts to provide direction and encouragement from Jehovah God. This book goes some way to showing that the contrary is in fact the case. Many accounts from former members of New York Bethel reveal that the members of the Governing Body live like kings, with nothing but the finest things. They do indeed enjoy reverence when they give special talks at various conventions around the world, with much excitement being generated at the prospect of seeing and hearing one. Furthermore, it is clear that the rank-and-file Witnesses are the ones who are slaves to the decrees of the Governing Body. The countless hours put into the preaching work and ever-demanding meeting and study schedule testify to this. Not only do individual Witnesses do all of this, they also pay for it with their own money. Each item of literature, whether it is a magazine, Bible, or CDROM[6] has a 'recommended donation' to cover the cost of production. It is expected that each Witness pay for the literature he takes for his use and for those used in the preaching work. However, that is only the bare minimum. The religion must grow, and therefore more money is needed

---

[6] One thing that stood out as interesting was the Watchtower Library CDROM. This disc contains all the printed study materials back to the 1960s (funny how they didn't go further back to the really embarrassing stuff). The disc had a donation amount of £10 and conveniently had the facility to install all content onto a person's computer, meaning the disc was only needed once. Seeing as the physical production cost of a CD is literally pennies, it was a little alarming to see the cost stated as £10, though obviously some work was required to compile the information into a single resource. It became apparent that many Brothers were getting a copy and installing it onto many other Brother's and Sister's computers. There were several talks given from the platform that stressed how important it was that each individual who wanted to use the Watchtower Library had to buy their own copy. This was claimed to be for Copyright reasons. However, when the Watchtower Society also makes claims that 'The Truth' should never be sold for profit, this approach seems questionable. Surely it would make sense for each congregation to obtain a copy and make it available to all members. This would save production and shipping costs. At £10 each and with most families buying the latest copy each year, a substantial amount of revenue is generated.

for building new Kingdom Halls and other Society projects. Each congregation supports and finances the running and maintenance costs of its own Hall. Who really is the Slave?

> *"No critical questions about leader, doctrine, or policy seen as legitimate"*

Cleverly, the Watchtower Society chooses mainly to focus on building trust in its followers as the sole path to salvation. They have created a system whereby any criticism instantly falls under the label of apostasy or the 'lies of Satan'. Since we have already discussed that aspect, we'll take a quick look at the claims the Governing body makes about itself.

> "There are many reasons why the slave class deserves our trust. Two outstanding reasons are: (1) Jehovah trusts the slave class. (2) Jesus also trusts the slave. Let us examine the evidence that both Jehovah God and Jesus Christ have complete confidence in the faithful and discreet slave." – *The Watchtower*, Feb 15th 2009, p.24-28.

The above paragraph is incredibly bold, but does nothing to prove that the Governing Body is in fact that slave. Instead it relies on a pre-established attachment between the two. The next quote (from the same article) goes even further.

> "Jesus referred to the composite body of his spirit-anointed followers on earth as "the faithful and discreet slave," or "the faithful steward." (Matt. 24:3, 45; Luke 12:42) As a group, the slave class has established an excellent record of "following the Lamb no matter where he goes." (*Read Revelation 14:4, 5.*) Its members remain virgins in a spiritual sense by not defiling themselves with the beliefs and practices of "Babylon the Great," the world empire of false religion. (Rev. 17:5) No doctrinal falsehood is "found in their mouths," and they remain "without blemish" from Satan's world." – *The Watchtower*, Feb 15th 2009, p.24-28.

As a Witness I would have read and nodded in complete agreement with this paragraph. Knowing what I do now, I find it shocking and actually shake my head in disbelief. Having studied the history and past teachings of the Watchtower Society my response to the statement that the Slave has "…an excellent record of 'following the Lamb no matter where he goes'" would be something along the lines of 'Well that Lamb has been to some crazy places then'. Quite frankly, I'd be right too.

In the literature there is no room for doubt that the Society is anything other than God's chosen messenger.

> *"No alternative belief systems viewed as legitimate, good, or useful"*

This is a frequent underlying topic in publications produced by the Watchtower Society. They have a constant battle to undermine *any* alternative belief system to further uphold their own, as the following quote shows:

> "Do we hear valueless things being uttered today? Yes. For example, some scientists say that evolutionary theory and scientific discoveries in other fields demonstrate that there is no longer any need to believe in God, that everything can be explained by natural processes. Should such proud statements concern us? Of course not! Human wisdom differs from divine wisdom. (1 Cor. 2:6, 7) However, we know that when human teachings contradict what God has revealed, it is *always* the human teachings that are wrong. (*Read Romans 3:4.*) Despite the progress of science in some fields, the Bible's assessment of human wisdom remains true: "The wisdom of this world is foolishness with God." Compared with the infinite wisdom of God, human reasoning is futile. —1 Cor. 3:18-20.
>
> Another example of valueless words is found among the religious leaders of Christendom. These claim to speak in God's name, but most of their utterances are not based on the Scriptures, and what

they say is basically worthless. Apostates too speak valueless words, claiming to have greater wisdom than the appointed "faithful and discreet slave." (Matt. 24:45-47) However, apostates speak their own wisdom, and their words are valueless, a stumbling block to any who might listen." – *The Watchtower*, 15th April 2008, p.3-7.

The objective of such articles is clear. The Watchtower Society poisons every alternative option in the minds of its adherents. The fallacy can be just as clearly seen when one unravels the argument. The Watchtower says that human wisdom is fatally inferior to God's. They have oversimplified things into a 'right verses wrong' scenario. God is always right, man is always wrong. The argument is then mirrored between so-called Apostates and the 'Faithful and Discreet Slave'. The heavily generalised statement puts Apostates in the place of fallible man, and the 'Faithful Slave' in place of God. This allows them to subtly attach themselves to the perfection, infallibility, and trustworthiness they claim He has. The problem here of course is that this 'Slave', the Governing Body is made up solely of mere humans. The previous chapter goes some way to showing how little input (any) God had in their decision-making.

When doctrinal changes are implemented, care is needed to introduce the new teaching(s) gently and tactfully, as people are attached to the current beliefs[7]. Witnesses refer to these changes as 'New Light'. The Watchtower explains:

"Go On Walking in the Path of Increasing Light

Accepting a change when it comes and adapting to it can be difficult," admits one longtime elder. What has helped him accept the many refinements he has witnessed in the 48 years that he has

---

[7] Current beliefs are *The Truth* after all.

been a Kingdom proclaimer? He answers: "Having the right attitude is the key. Refusing to accept a refinement is to be left behind as the organization moves ahead. If I find myself in a situation where changes seem hard to accept, I reflect on Peter's words to Jesus: 'Lord, whom shall we go away to? You have sayings of everlasting life.' Then I ask myself, 'Where shall I go away to—out there into the darkness of the world?' This helps me to hold firmly to God's organization." —John 6:68.

The world around us is certainly in dense darkness. As Jehovah continues to shed light on his people, the gap between them and those of the world keeps on widening. What does this light do for us? Well, just as shining a spotlight on a pothole on a dark roadway does not remove the hole, light from God's Word does not remove pitfalls. Yet, divine light surely helps us to avoid them so that we can continue walking in the path of increasing light. Let us, then, continue to pay attention to Jehovah's prophetic word, "as to a lamp shining in a dark place." – *The Watchtower,* Feb 15th 2006, p.30.

These two paragraphs contain a wealth of powerful and manipulative information. The programming is clear when the sentences are broken down. The article admits that there have been many 'refinements' (read 'key doctrinal changes') over the years. However, if one has an issue with any of these changes (past, present or future) it is the individual's attitude that is wrong, not the Society. The reader is then subjected to subtle psychological and emotional blackmail by the threat of being 'left behind' if they refuse to accept the change. The article slyly then reminds the reader that they're either in 'The Truth' or in 'The World'. If they get left behind, there are no longer part of 'The Truth' and therefore default to the only available alternative, 'The World'. Everything in 'The World' is painted as dismal and dire.

What is of particular interest is the way even in just two paragraphs the reader is conditioned that these changes are normal and to be expected. A positive spin is next applied as 'changes' are redefined as 'refinements'. The reader is made to feel guilty if they question such refinements, since refinements are a good thing. The article fails to clarify that is the human interpretation that changes, not 'God's Word'. The reader is not allowed to think that he can follow God without following the Watchtower Society, since they are blurred as if they were one and the same.

The articles in *The Watchtower* magazine and other Society publications are frequent, with similarly clever pieces of programming propaganda. It is quite frightening to see how in just small excerpts we can see elements of Behaviour, Information, Thought, and Emotional control being used.

Emotional Control

One of the most powerful methods of control over people is the use of emotions, which can often easily overrule logic and rationality. Two of the most powerful emotions are fear and guilt. Would you be surprised if most Witnesses suffer from above average levels of these emotions? I can truthfully state that I have not only experienced them myself, but have seen them in so many others, as they've battled 'Satan's system' in service to the Watchtower Society.

The Emotional Control section of the B.I.T.E. model almost mirrors the life of a Jehovah's Witness:

Excessive Use of Guilt

"Who you are (not living up to your potential)"

Witnesses are always trying to be better people and aspire to put on a 'Christ-like personality'. When they inevitably fail to meet Jesus' 'perfect standards', they naturally feel guilt, frustration, and their sense of self worth suffers. They will pray for forgiveness for their imperfections and trust that Jehovah will overlook them. However, a person must endeavour to imitate Jesus' perfect example at all times, and therefore are bound to regularly fail. Salvation is never a guarantee and one must always look to make the most of every available opportunity to spread the 'Good news of God's kingdom'. A Witness would regularly feel guilty if they missed an opportunity to tell someone about their beliefs.

"Your family"

As a Witness, your only real family are your 'spiritual Brothers and Sisters'. Flesh and blood relatives (if not Witnesses) are part of 'The World' and therefore cannot be viewed the same as your fellow servants of Jehovah. Furthermore, only Witnesses uphold the high moral standards that Jehovah has set out. Any non-Witnesses fall into the category of 'Bad Association'. There often is a huge barrier present in families who are a mix of Witnesses and 'Worldly People'.

"Your past"

Whether a Witness was born into 'The Truth' or joined at some point in their life, they will have varying degrees of guilt over past wrongs. Those who were raised as Jehovah's Witnesses would have inevitable guilt from past errors and sins (even very minor ones). These would include times they gave a 'bad witness', which would be any time they did something that brought the religion into disrepute (i.e. by swearing or lying etc). Young males no doubt battle with guilt over sexual thoughts and masturbation (of course this would also affect females, but perhaps to a lesser extent). This probably explains why several chapters in the Watchtower Society's 'Questions Young People Ask' book deal with this very subject.

Witnesses who joined the religion later on in life often find themselves battling guilt over sins they committed before they were baptised. Also they will have had a battle on their hands trying to bring their personality in line with Watchtower standards. Someone who routinely swore for example would have a more difficult time trying to desist from doing so. Though many of these 'failings' may seem petty or insignificant, they are a big thing to a Jehovah's Witness. Individuals will suffer to varying degrees however, based on how they view such actions on a personal level and how seriously they take the religion in general.

"Your affiliations"

Who you associate with is highly important as a Witness. Anyone who is not an earnest servant of Jehovah could fall under the label of 'Bad Association'. People of 'The World' are by definition bad associates.

'The World' is the Witness term for referring to everything and everyone outside the Jehovah's Witness religion. It's not a positive phrase, rather it is used distinguish everything a Witness should be from everything a Witness shouldn't. From the religion's point of view, you are either in the 'Truth' or in the 'World', which belongs to the Devil. Witnesses are strongly discouraged from forming any friendships with people outside the religion, as they are to be 'no part of the world'. This is particularly damaging to children who want to be accepted by their schoolmates, yet are unable to socialise or made to feel guilty if they do. This is justified by a desire to avoid 'bad association' which in a general sense is wise. However, no-one want's their children to 'fall in with the wrong crowd', and a little common sense and education will help a child to make good choices. The Jehovah's Witness attitude encourages mistrust of everyone who is outside the religion.

> "Further, **the desire of young people to participate in school sports events, which can easily lead to bad association**, can be strong. "I love sports," says a young sister named Tanya. "The coaches in school were always trying to get me to play on the team. It was hard to refuse."

How can you help your children to meet their many challenges? Jehovah commissioned parents to provide guidance for their offspring. (Prov. 22:6; Eph. 6:4) The goal of God-fearing parents is to develop in their children's hearts a desire to obey Jehovah. (Prov. 6:20-23) **In that way, children will be motivated to resist the world's pressures** even when their parents are not watching."
- *The Watchtower,* 15th Jan 2010, p.16-20.

Even basic after-school activities are strongly discouraged for fear of 'bad association' with 'worldly people'. This strict standard is expected of adults as well as children. Such is the level of separation required of *all* Jehovah's Witnesses.

Excessive Use of Fear

"Fear of thinking independently"

This is particularly strong since it is a term actively used by the Watchtower. Articles regularly are printed that outline the dangers of 'Independent Thinking' or developing an 'Independent Spirit'. Such demonising of these buzzwords naturally instils fear of acquiring them as a trait or even being labelled as an 'Independent Thinker'. One would also actively avoid associating with any Witness who had shown such behaviour. In fact Witnesses take pride in viewing themselves as humble sheep, which follow their leader wherever he goes[8].

"Fear of the "outside" world" & "Fear of enemies"

Everything in the outside world is believed to be under Satan's control and therefore fear follows naturally. Satan and his army of demons are out to trick Witnesses into committing sins, viewing Apostate or

---

[8] See the next chapter for an overview of the book 'Shepherd the Flock of God", published by Watchtower Bible & Tract Society.

demonic information, or having serious doubts about the truth of their beliefs.

With the whole world under the Devil's control, enemies are everywhere. Anything with a demonic or spiritistic theme or undertone is a doorway to allowing demons access to your psyche. Whether it's the Harry Potter or Lord of the Rings books and films, or a horoscope in a newspaper, the demons are out to get you. Fear is all but guaranteed.

Another keyword in Witness lingo is 'Fear of Man'. There is regular council given at the Kingdom Halls as to combatting fear of the people of the world. Fear is expected from relatively small things such as mocking at school, work, or out in the door-to-door field service. Fear of man is also apparent with stories in the Watchtower Yearbooks of Brothers and Sisters facing violence and persecution in foreign countries from other religious groups and governments. These are foretold to become worse as the end of the system draws near. Fear is instilled at every opportunity while the Watchtower holds itself up as the only path to freedom from such strife.

> *"Fear of losing one's salvation", "of leaving the group" & "disapproval"*

All Witnesses are afraid of not being good enough or having not done enough to prove themselves worthy of the paradise reward. There is a conditioned fear against Jehovah God's disapproval. He is watching everything we do, everything we say, and even everything we think. We are firmly in Orwell's *'Nineteen Eighty-Four'* territory now, with every thought scrutinised and judged.

Fear of leaving is evident, as the resultant shunning policy means that a person is cut-off from all their friends, their family (if they are Witnesses) and their whole social support network. A person is abandoned unless they humbly return to the fold and work to prove their regret over their wrongdoing.

> *"Extremes of emotional highs and lows."*

This is an interesting point that I had not considered before reading Hassan's work. Having thought about it for a while, it is clear how this does apply to the Witnesses. When at the Kingdom Hall there is almost frantic bliss as everyone makes a special effort to be as Christian as possible. The smiles and warm greetings fill the Hall. Even when groups meet for field service or a gathering for a meal this same atmosphere blossoms. It is an emotional high that instils in the minds of followers that they really are 'in The Truth'. Conversely, many Witnesses also suffer from depression and other mental disorders as many psychological professionals have noted. People who are normally social outcasts can find acceptance and form friendships within the loving group, provided they conform to the rules of the Watchtower Society. Furthermore, with the arrival of Armageddon being endlessly 'just around the corner', many Witnesses begin to feel tired and depressed. Their hope lies purely in the intervention of God to sort the world's problems. As a result, their day-to-day lives can often become a 'low' with the peaks of 'highs' developing at Witness' gatherings where rejuvenation with like-minded believers takes place.

> *"Ritual and often public confession of 'sins'."*

Although confession boxes are not present at Kingdom Halls, there definitely is a 'Cult of Confession' present. Witnesses are supposed to challenge a Brother or Sister if they believe that person has committed a sin that needs addressing. They are to urge that person to go to the Elders and confess the wrongdoing. If that individual fails to heed your council, you are to bring along another who would act as a witness to the council being repeated. If the individual still refuses to change his ways or speak to the congregation Elders about the matter, you are to report it to them yourself. Even in this type of situation, several people become aware of an individual's sin(s), making it nearly a public affair. Witnesses though have never properly applied this procedure in my experience. Far too often I have seen Elders being informed of people's actions (whether truly right or wrong) including myself. I also know of many others in different congregations that have seen this same practice. This 'Ratting' behaviour operates as a level of surveillance that rivals aspects of North Korean society.

Whilst this 'spy & rat' mentality works well, it doesn't beat the self-confessions of those who are guilt-ridden. Witnesses routinely go to the Elders for advice on difficulties they have got themselves into, including deeply personal subjects. Naturally one has to confess to wrongdoing in order to give an Elder (or group of Elders) a full account of what happened. Any questions asked by the Elders must be answered openly and honestly, no matter how personal they are. To lie to the Elders is to lie to Jehovah, and therefore utterly reprehensible. Confessions are a frequent occurrence; the rationale is that Jehovah knows and sees all, so to hide a sin from the Elders is to put ones salvation in jeopardy.

If one has committed a serious sin and has shown genuine repentance for their error, they will face a Judicial Hearing but may not be expelled from the congregation (disfellowshipped). They will however get a 'Public Reproof', which means an announcement will be made at the Kingdom Hall that ''X' has been reproved'. Everyone in the congregation will then know that this individual has committed some serious wrong, but they won't know what the offence was[9].

---

[9] The prevalence of gossip within congregations means that often people's offences are in fact made common knowledge.

Phobia Indoctrination

> "Programming of irrational fears of ever leaving the group or even questioning the leader's authority...
>
> a. No happiness or fulfillment "outside"of the group
>
> b. Terrible consequences will take place if you leave: "hell"; "demon possession"; "incurable diseases"; "accidents"; "suicide"; "insanity"; "10,000 reincarnations"; etc.
>
> c. Shunning of leave takers. Fear of being rejected by friends, peers, and family.
>
> d. Never a legitimate reason to leave. From the group's perspective, people who leave are: "weak;" "undisciplined;" "unspiritual;" "worldly;" "brainwashed by family, counselors;" seduced by money, sex, rock and roll."

I think it has been made very clear how Jehovah's Witnesses view a life outside 'The Truth' as hopeless and deeply undesirable. In addition to facing the shunning and labels as worldly, weak, godless, or selfish, one also expects to be destroyed by God at Armageddon unless he can return to the flock. While he is 'in the World' he has lost Jehovah's blessing and his spiritual protection. He is now part of Satan's system and fully vulnerable to his attacks.

Leaving 'The Truth'

> "What if we have a relative or a close friend who is disfellowshipped? Now our loyalty is on the line, not to that person, but to God. Jehovah is watching us to see whether we will abide by his command not to have contact with anyone who is disfellowshipped." - *The Watchtower*, Apr 15th 2012, p.12.

It is clear that one cannot leave the religion without serious consequences. The psychological trauma starts when a person begins to have doubts and continues right through to their eventual escape. However, the battle is not yet over. If that person makes the decision to remain outside the religion, he must rebuild his life, restructure his belief system, and form a new social circle. His programmed thinking patterns and view of the world must be totally rewritten. To this end, he must accept that Jehovah's Witnesses do not in fact have 'The Truth', and allow the concepts that once held him captive to fall apart.

CHAPTER 7

A CONCEPT FALLS APART

Once a Jehovah's Witnesses learns that they are following what the Governing Body says, rather than the Bible, it becomes easier to break free from their authority and control. The Witness' viewpoint is that the Governing Body is Jehovah's mouthpiece. Each new teaching that is presented comes from Jehovah God, through his visible organisation on Earth: the Governing Body. Should a small correction be needed, it would be in the form of Jehovah refining his chosen people before the great day of judgement. However, as one learns the history, deceptions, and general fallacies, it quickly becomes apparent that this is not God's chosen organisation after all. Aside from whether or not a God even exists.

Jehovah's 'Channel of Communication'

The Governing Body of Jehovah's Witnesses claims to be directed by Jehovah's Holy Spirit. They claim to be the 'Faithful and Discreet Slave' mentioned in Matthew 24:45-47:

> "Who really is the faithful and discreet slave whom his master appointed over his domestics, to give them their food at the proper time? Happy is that slave if his master on arriving finds him doing so. Truly I say to YOU, He will appoint him over all his belongings."

In addition to being the faithful slave, they also claim to be directed exclusively by God's Holy Spirit.

> "Consider, too, the fact that **Jehovah's organization alone, in all the earth, is directed by God's holy spirit** or active force." - *The Watchtower,* Jul 1st 1973, p.402.

> "**The Watchtower is not the instrument of any man or set of men, nor is it published according to the whims of men. No man's opinion is expressed in The Watchtower. God feeds his own people**, and surely God uses those who love and serve him according to his own will. Those who oppose The Watchtower are not capable of discerning the truth that God is giving to the children of his organization, and this is the very strongest proof that such opposers are not of God's organization." - *The Watchtower,* Nov 1st 1931, p.327.

> "...**the 'greatly diversified wisdom of God' can become known only through Jehovah's channel of communication**, the faithful and discreet slave." - *The Watchtower,* Oct 1st 1994, p.8.

As mentioned in chapter one, there is a discrepancy between the slave class (the 144,000 anointed Witnesses) and the Governing Body. Witnesses don't follow the remnant of the 144,000 (despite this being the understanding of scripture); they follow only the direction of the Governing Body (who are also anointed). The remaining anointed ones serve alongside regular Witnesses, without any authority or influence.

Oddly however, despite being 'Spirit Directed', the Governing Body claims that all anointed Witnesses (which would include themselves) do not have any special insights.

> "However, genuine anointed Christians do not demand special attention. **They do not believe that their being of the anointed gives them special 'insights,'** beyond what even some experienced members of the great crowd may have. **They do not believe that they necessarily have more holy spirit than their companions** of the other sheep have; nor do they expect special treatment or claim that their partaking of the emblems places them above the appointed elders in the congregation." - *The Watchtower,* May 1st 2007, p.23.

The question that should rightly be asked is, 'How are the anointed Governing Body acting as Jehovah's Channel of Communication without special insights?' It's an interesting question indeed, and has thus far gone unanswered. However, the latest 'New Light' reveals a significant change in belief. It would appear that it is the Governing Body alone that are the 'Faithful Slave', and not the collective 144,000 anointed Witnesses as was previously taught for decades. This solves the aforementioned problem, but raises three further issues. The first is an obvious question: How do they know that it only refers to them? God has not updated the Bible for the twenty-first century, and no new scrolls have been found. Secondly, if this was a new revelation, why has God waited till now to correct his chosen organisation? This is especially important considering they profess to be teaching 'The Truth'. Thirdly, if this change is a correction or refinement by God, then it meant he was happy for a completely wrong belief to be taught as truth for many years. The whole concept here is, at the very least, unconvincing.

The Truth ... That Changes

The religion's beliefs are referred to as 'The Truth'. Unfortunately however, 'The Truth' has changed multiple times on multiple key doctrines. If 'The Truth' has had to change, it clearly wasn't always the truth. Yet followers were expected to obey and believe false things, until they were later 'corrected'.

If an individual felt strongly enough that some belief or teaching was wrong and refused to change his mind, he would be removed from the religion and shunned by his friends and family. If later "New Light' was discovered and that particular teaching was changed, would that individual be contacted and reinstated without question? No! He would still be outcast, despite having been right all along. He would be expected to appeal to the congregation Elders to come back, and show genuine repentance for his lack of faith in the organisation and Jehovah. Remember, some of these teachings affect Witnesses on a life or death basis. Trivialities aside, this is a highly important issue.

The frankly embarrassing history of the Watchtower Society, replete with mistakes, cover-ups, and contradictions only serves to testify against its claim that it alone is God's chosen organisation. The Bible itself sums it up rather well.

> "However, the prophet who presumes to speak in my name a word that I have not commanded him to speak or who speaks in the name of other gods, **that prophet must die**. And in case you should say in your heart: "How shall we know the word that Jehovah has not spoken?" **when the prophet speaks in the name of Jehovah and the word does not occur** or come true, that is the word that Jehovah did not speak. With presumptuousness the prophet spoke it." - *Deu 18:20-22*.

'Secret' Elder's Handbook

Most regular Jehovah's Witnesses are not aware that the Elders of each congregation have a secret handbook at their disposal. It contains the official rules and regulations that the Watchtower Society requires Elders to enforce. This book outlines the procedures for handling misconduct from 'minor' offences all the way up to paedophilia. I have heard of Elders claiming this book not to be a secret publication, yet the letter that accompanies it makes clear that the opposite is true.

> "We would like to emphasize the importance of keeping these new textbooks secured and confidential, both before and after they are distributed. The textbooks should not be left on tops of desks or in other places where they are easily accessible by family members or other individuals. The information is designed for use by the elders only, and other individuals should not have any opportunity to read the information." - *Letter to All Bodies of Elders,* Aug 23rd 2010, p.1.

(See Appendix 'F' for the full scan of this letter)

In addition, this follow up letter was sent after requests were made by individual Elders to have the new book spiral bound.

> "There is no objection if an elder personally spiral binds or laminates his own textbook or does so for other elders. If he has another baptized brother who is not an elder do the work for him, the elder must watch while the work is being done. Outside companies, unbelievers, or sisters are not permitted to do this work. The material in the book is confidential, and confidentiality must be preserved." - *Letter to All Bodies of Elders,* Octo 7th 2010, p.1.

(See Appendix 'G' for the full scan of this letter)

Regardless of any individual claims, it is clear that this book is intended to be secret. However, it can be found in PDF format online with relative ease (from unofficial sources). The question that arises is: What does it contain that requires concealment? The reality is that much of the book is general and sensible instruction, and is far from a thrilling read. However, there is still reason for concern. Seven of the twelve chapters are dedicated to the handling of 'Judicial Matters', that is, how the Elders deal with wrongdoing in the congregation.

The first chapter is concluded with pleasantly idealistic description of the role of Elders.

> "To be an effective elder, you must care for Jehovah's precious sheep in the same way that he does – with loving-kindness, impartiality, and merciful judgement. Jehovah's people and, more important, Jehovah and his Son greatly appreciate your diligent efforts in behalf of the congregation. We pray for Jehovah's blessing to 'be with the spirit you show.'" - *Shepherd the Flock of God*, 2010, p.9.

As gentle and loving as this appears to be, a few areas of the book when carefully analysed raise more than an eyebrow. We will briefly examine a few examples relating to 'judicial matters'. Chapter seven of the 'Flock' book describes the procedure for judging an individual. It outlines that accused Witnesses are not permitted to have anyone sit with them for moral support. Rather, they must face the committee of three to five Elders alone. In addition, recording devices are not allowed. The secrecy surrounding these court-like hearings is emphasised throughout the publication. There are also repeated and emphasised instructions to handle all matters orally (p.24 p.82 p.100 p.101). The Elders are expected to put things in writing only as a last resort. Yet when requesting details from the accused or other Witnesses, they routinely expect written confirmation, which is to my mind, hypocritical *(p.93 p.99 p.103)*.

We start to find more worrisome elements as we come to the subject of apostasy. Apostasy is a term that strikes terror into the mind of the average Jehovah's Witness. An Apostate is someone who has not only turned their back on Jehovah, but is actively working against him and his organisation. Witnesses are instructed to avoid Apostates at all costs. Chapter five of the 'Flock' book outlines the offences that would qualify one as an Apostate.

"Apostasy is a standing away from true worship! a falling away defection, rebellion, abandonment. It includes the following:

- Celebrating false religious holidays: (Ex. 32: 4-6; Jer. 7:16-19) Not all holidays directly involve false religion and require judicial action.

- Participation in interfaith activities: (2 Cor. 6:14, 15, 17, 18) Apostate acts include bowing before altars and images and sharing in false religious songs and prayers.

- Deliberately spreading teachings contrary to Bible truth as taught by Jehovah's Witnesses: (Acts 21:21, ftn.; 2 John 7, 9, 10) Any with sincere doubts should be helped. Firm, loving counsel should be given. (2 Tim. 2: 16-19, 23-26; Jude 22, 23) If one obstinately is speaking about or deliberately spreading false teachings, this may be or may lead to apostasy. If there is no response after a first and a second admonition, a judicial committee should be formed.

- Causing divisions and promoting sects: This would be deliberate action disrupting the unity of the congregation or undermining the confidence of the brothers in Jehovah's arrangement. It may involve or lead to apostasy.

- Continuing in employment that makes one an accomplice to or a promoter of false worship would subject one to disfellowshipping after being allowed a reasonable amount of time, perhaps up to six months, to make the needed adjustments.

- The practice of spiritism.

- Idolatry: (1 Cor. 6:9, 10; 10:14) Idolatry includes the use of images, including pictures, in false religious worship." - *Shepherd the Flock of God*, 2010, p.65-66.

The prohibition against getting involved in religious holidays applies to most popular celebrations such as Christmas, Halloween, Easter, New Year, Birthdays, Carnivals, Harvest Festival, Mother's, Father's, and even Valentine's Day and Guy Fawkes. These are all viewed as displeasing to Jehovah, and are to be strictly avoided. The result of this avoidance is clear as Witnesses are further separated from 'people of the world'. Despite living amongst non-witnesses, they are mentally segregated from society, as we will later see.

The second example given relates to interfaith activities. This includes sharing in any way with any other religion. This would include going to another church that is not a Kingdom Hall of Jehovah's Witnesses, singing hymns at school, closing your eyes during a non-witness prayer (which signifies sharing), participating in interfaith debates, and anything similar.

The third example is interestingly worded. One would expect it to read: 'Deliberately spreading teachings contrary to Bible truth'. However they have added: '...as taught by Jehovah's Witnesses'. This changes the sin from going against God, to going against the Watchtower Society. The point is further made in the forth example of apostasy, which talks about 'undermining the confidence of the brothers in Jehovah's arrangement'. The word 'arrangement' is interchangeable with 'organisation', which itself is interchangeable with 'Watchtower Society'. Jehovah's Witnesses are not permitted to voice anything critical of the Society, because any such expression would amount to apostasy. Likewise, they would strictly avoid reading anything or even thinking anything that is critical of the beliefs and teachings that come from the Watchtower. This is heavy information and thought control.

The sixth point rather speaks for itself but the seventh is short and sweet. The practice of spiritism could involve many things, and the Watchtower specifically mentions a few and what to do about them should you find yourself in a difficult situation. Without going into too much detail (as I feel a tangent coming on), films that feature demons, ghosts, and sorcery are off limits. I remember hearing from the platform of the assembly hall that the Lord of the Rings, Harry Potter, and even Avatar films were to be avoided due to spiritualistic dangers. There is even a recently released Witness DVD animation that features a young Witness child playing with a toy wizard that a school friend had given him. His mother explains the dangers of playing with such a toy and how displeasing it is to Jehovah God. The child gets rid of the toy and finds his life is better as a result. Similar avoidance applies to fortune-tellers, horoscopes, Ouija boards, fortune cookies, and similar. The fear associated with such 'dangerous material' is a distinct part of the control over members.

The last example of apostasy refers to idolatry, and specifically mentions the use of images in what it calls 'false worship'. The admonition to avoid images (which includes items like the crucifx etc.) acts as a further distinction of separation in the minds of 'rank and file' Witnesses. To ordinary believers, they are different to all other religions of the world because of such 'standards'. To conclude on the point of apostasy, we will look at a quote from the Watchtower magazine that outlines the clear viewpoint that all Witnesses should follow.

> "...we need to guard against succumbing to apostasy, a sin that would make us unfit to glorify God. Let us therefore have nothing to do with apostates or anyone who claims to be a brother but who is dishonoring God. This should be the case even if he is a family member. We are not benefited by trying to refute the arguments of apostates or those who are critical of Jehovah's organization. In fact, it is spiritually dangerous and improper to peruse their information, whether it appears in written form or it is found on the Internet." - *The Watchtower,* 15th May 2012, p.25.

The article bundles people who make criticism of the Watchtower Society with the 'evil Apostates'. Such labelling creates an automatic block in the mind of any Witness. They also naturally begin to fear critical thoughts, no matter how small, in case they should become such a dreaded individual. The instruction not to even 'refute the arguments of Apostates' or indeed anyone who is critical of the Society, allows the Witness to simply ignore the information. They are in fact to flee from such 'wickedness', as their eternal life depends on it.

The *Shepherd the Flock of God* book also contains concerning information regarding the handling of sexual abuse of children. The rules regarding what constitutes adequate evidence for judicial action includes the following:

> "Even though a Christian has accused of wrongdoing serious enough to require judicial action, **a judicial committee should not be formed unless the wrongdoing has been established.**
>
> - Confession. (Admission of wrongdoing), either written or orally, may be accepted as conclusive proof without corroborating evidence. (Josh. 7:19) There must be two witnesses to a confession, and the confession must be clear and unambiguous. For example, a statement from a married Christian that his mate is "Scripturally free" would not by itself viewed a confession of adultery.
>
> - A guilty plea entered in a court by a Christian as part of a plea bargain, perhaps on the advice of an attorney so as to avoid the possibility of a harsher sentence, would generally not in itself be viewed as an admission of guilt in the congregation.
>
> - There must be **two or three eyewitness**, not just people repeating hearsay; no action can be taken if there is only one witness. -- Deut. 19:15; John 8:17
>
> - If there are two or three **witnesses to the same kind of wrongdoing but each one is witness to a separate incident**, the elders can consider their testimony. While such evidence is acceptable to establish guilt, it is

> preferable to have two witnesses to the same occurrence of wrongdoing. - *Shepherd the Flock of God,* 2010, p.71-72.

Of particular interest are points three and four that outline the 'more than one witness' rule. This is extremely important, since how often would there be two or more witnesses to an incident of paedophilia or domestic violence? Yet these are abhorrent crimes. This policy therefore fosters a level of protection for such ones. Importantly, the 'Flock' book does specifically discuss child molestation, and has the following to say:

> "19. Child abuse is a crime. **Never suggest to anyone that they should not report an allegation of child abuse to the police or other authorities.** If you are asked, make it clear that whether to report the matter to the authorities or not is a personal decision for each individual to make and that there are no congregation sanctions for either decision. Elders will not criticize anyone who reports such an allegation to the authorities. If the victim wishes to make a report, it is his or her absolute right to do so." - *Shepherd the Flock of God*, 2010, p.131-132.

Shockingly the admonition is only to NEVER suggest that someone should NOT go to the police when sexual abuse of children takes place. What is mortifying is the complete betrayal of the moral obligation someone in a position of authority has in this situation. Namely, to tell the person to go to the police! It is deeply troubling that this is not the case within this important handbook. Upon examination, it seems likely the only reason this line is in place is to legally protect the Society from blame, rather than to protect children.

In addition to the above, there is also a clause that enables someone to 'get away with' serious acts by waiting until a much later time to reveal them.

> "...if the **immorality or other serious wrongdoing** occurred **more than a few years ago** and the individual is genuinely repentant

and recognizes that he should have come forward immediately when he sinned, **good counsel by elders may be sufficient.**" - *Shepherd the Flock of God*, 2010, p.74.

How can this possibly be an acceptable rule for an organisation that claims to adhere to strict 'cleanliness'? It is another example of a corrupt man-made system that enacts autocratic control of its subjects, whilst simultaneously teaching and enforcing contradictory rules and regulations as it sees fit.

The Reality at the Top

Reading 'Crisis of Conscience' (Raymond Franz, 1983) reveals a multitude of disturbing facts about how things really work at the Watchtower headquarters. One issue that particularly stood out was the two-thirds majority requirement. At the time, Brother Franz was a member of the Governing Body, of which there were eighteen in total. If a proposal were made to change a teaching, the Body would hold a vote. If there was not a two-thirds majority voting in favour of the change, then the old teaching remained. Brother Franz remarks how he wondered what Brothers and Sisters would feel if they knew that the majority of Governing Body members felt something was wrong, but because a two-thirds majority had not been reached, the old teaching remained in place, time and time again.

One point that is worth considering is why a vote would be needed at all. If God's spirit were directing their decisions, a vote would surely not be necessary. Are Jehovah's Witnesses following God, or men?

Further reading of 'Crisis of Conscience' (Raymond Franz, 1983) reveals details of various power struggles and waves of disfellowshipping that took place to keep the current leadership intact. Perhaps in your journey through my book you have detected a level of anger or bitterness toward the Watchtower Society. You are not wrong. I certainly am upset about what happened to me and what was hidden from me. Reading the pages of Brother Franz's book however, there is no such animosity to detect. His sincerity and yearning for truth shines through. Reading how he was treated as he was conspired against to be ousted was deeply saddening. He was no troublemaker; rather his earnest efforts were to make the Society better, and to make the lives of the Brothers and Sisters better. He had a real love of truth and sought it with genuineness. He describes how the Governing Body sessions were mainly a discussion of Watchtower policy. Even though scriptures were sometimes presented, the policy took precedent over scripture. This was to him, as it was to me, a far cry from the way things are portrayed in the literature presented to the congregations.

Blood Transfusions

> "Today, faithful servants of God firmly resolve to follow his direction regarding blood. They will not eat it in any form. Nor will they accept blood for medical reasons. They are sure that the Creator of blood knows what is best for them." - *What Does the Bible Really Teach?* p.131.

The policy to refuse blood transfusions has resulted in many deaths of Jehovah's Witnesses over the years, has attracted much attention from the media and has been the cause of a lot of verbal abuse, particularly whilst participating in the door to door work, the mildest of which might indeed be 'You let your children die!'. This statement is indeed true; a Witness would most certainly allow their child to die instead of giving them a blood transfusion. It would not be easy of course, utterly devastating in fact. Only someone who has experienced that kind of loss can truly attest to the grief felt. I imagine the mixture of emotional turmoil that must plague parents who lost a child in this way can only be made worse by the guilt. Such guilt would stem from not doing everything to save the life that is perhaps more precious to you than your own. Jehovah's Witnesses have many rationalisations for this aspect of their beliefs. Much if not all of which has been provided by the Watchtower Bible & Tract Society, led by its Governing Body, the leadership of Jehovah's Witnesses. The doctrine is based on the following isolated scriptures:

> "Only flesh with its soul—its blood—YOU must not eat." – *Genesis 9:4.*

> "As for any man of the house of Israel or some alien resident who is residing as an alien in YOUR midst who eats any sort of blood, I shall certainly set my face against the soul that is eating the blood, and I shall indeed cut him off from among his people." – *Leviticus 17:10.*

> Simply be firmly resolved not to eat the blood, because the blood is the soul and you must not eat the soul with the flesh. – *Deuteronomy 12:23.*

> "…keep abstaining from things sacrificed to idols and from blood and from things strangled and from fornication. If YOU carefully keep yourselves from these things, YOU will prosper. Good health to YOU!" – *Acts 15:28.*

Even with the poorest of Biblical support for such a teaching, each Witness is required fill out and sign an Advanced Medical Directive and to give a copy to their doctor and a copy to the congregation Elders for them to keep on file. They'll also need a smaller copy to place in their wallet or purse so that if they are unconscious the emergency services will be unable to legally give them blood. If they have children they'll need to get similar card signed for them to carry around at all times, to prevent them from receiving blood in an emergency also.

In families that are not all Jehovah's Witnesses, extreme disagreement is likely in serious medical situations. This is commonly due to the opposing views held regarding the use of blood. As you can imagine, serious rifts can form between Witness and non-Witness members, especially if a person dies as a result of refusing a blood transfusion.

Jehovah: A God of Love?

Jehovah's Witnesses view their god like a loving perfect father. He is kind, just, powerful, and merciful. As imperfect humans, we deserve death (having inherited the original sin of Adam). By Jehovah's great mercy, he has sacrificed the life of his son so that we may one day be restored to perfection. We are indebted to him beyond words for his mercy and must praise and worship him where possible, every moment of every day.

It was Richard Dawkins that got me thinking by putting it somewhat differently:

> "The God of the Old Testament is arguably the most unpleasant character in all fiction: jealous and proud of it; a petty, unjust, unforgiving control-freak; a vindictive, bloodthirsty ethnic cleanser; a misogynistic, homophobic, racist, infanticidal, genocidal, filicidal, pestilential, megalomaniacal, sadomasochistic, capriciously malevolent bully." - *The God Delusion*, p.51.

Reading those words helped me to realise there is actually more bad in the Bible than good. Jehovah in the Old Testament was a warmonger, all too ready to destroy whole nations, including women, children, and even animals. Not to mention the sanctioning of human slavery. Apart from the gentler gospels in the New Testament, he, if it were believed, is preparing for the War of Armageddon. It is expected to be an apocalyptic war that will bring untold pain and destruction to the Earth, along with the death of billions of people.

Revelation in Evolution

The Watchtower Society is very good at poisoning every other religion in the minds of its adherents. When you believe that your religion is the only true one, your loyalties are firmly rooted. To you, other religions are laughable in what they teach and believe. However, once you come to realise that the Jehovah's Witness religion is no different really (sometimes worse) than all these others, you may start to ponder on the very existence of God.

If like myself you accepted the Watchtower Society's version of science, you likely would dismiss the theory of evolution as a myth or even a tool of Satan. However, a proper education in the mechanics and evidence supporting the theory will open a whole world of new understanding. One point I must mention is that the truth of evolution does not disprove the existence of God. It does however prove the Watchtower Society to be wrong and deceitful. Their flagrant use of pseudo-science creationist reasoning, and out of context quote mining, serves to further discredit them. They actually have the audacity to deny being creationists at all.

"ARE JEHOVAH'S WITNESSES CREATIONISTS?

Jehovah's Witnesses believe the creation account as recorded in the Bible book of Genesis. However, Jehovah's Witnesses are not what you might think of as creationists. Why not? First, many creationists believe that the universe and the earth and all life on it were created in six 24-hour days some 10,000 years ago. This, however, is *not* what the Bible teaches. Also, creationists have embraced many doctrines that lack support in the Bible. Jehovah's Witnesses base their religious teachings solely on God's Word." - *Awake!* Sep 2006, p.3.

This article is very misleading. Firstly it ignores the fact that two types of creationist exist. Jehovah's Witnesses are 'Old Earth Creationists' because they believe the planet Earth was created over an unspecified period of time. The paragraph only mentions 'Young Earth Creationists' that believe the Earth was created between 6000 – 10,000 years ago, contradicting scientific evidence in favour of a literal biblical understanding. The article continues to accuse creationists of embracing non-biblical doctrines, but gives no examples or evidence. It then goes on to attach an irrelevant criticism regarding political involvement.

"Furthermore, in some lands the term "creationist" is synonymous with Fundamentalist groups that actively engage in politics. These groups attempt to pressure politicians, judges, and educators into adopting laws and teachings that conform to the creationists' religious code." - *Awake!* Sep 2006, p.3.

Whilst in 'some' lands this may be true, it is a fallacy to generalise a large group of people in such a way. It is akin to saying that Jehovah's Witnesses are not religious because in some lands religion is the cause of wars.

Misrepresenting Science

Jehovah's Witnesses are crippled with incorrect information regarding even the most basic understanding of the theory of evolution. This gives them a distorted view of reality, and bolsters the opinion that evolution is a ridiculous notion.

> "**Organic evolution is the theory that the first living organism developed from lifeless matter**. Then, as it reproduced, it is said, it changed into different kinds of living things, ultimately producing all forms of plant and animal life that have ever existed on this earth. All of this is said to have been accomplished without the supernatural intervention of a Creator. Some persons endeavor to blend belief in God with evolution, saying that God created by means of evolution, that he brought into existence the first primitive life forms and that then higher life forms, including man, were produced by means of evolution. *Not a Bible teaching.*" - *Reasoning from the Scriptures,* p.121.

The first sentence in the above paragraph is an utterly false statement. Evolution only relates to life already in existence. Life arising from non-living matter is a completely different scientific theory called 'Abiogenesis'. What's worrying is the Watchtower Society cannot even get the basic definition of evolution correct. It is either a mistake, or more likely (in my opinion) a deliberate attempt to confuse the matter.

Since 1985, Jehovah's Witnesses used their publication 'Life – How Did it Get Here? By Evolution or by Creation?' as their main tool on the subject. This book has been openly denounced for it's misuse of quotes and is frequently accused of using typically flawed creationist reasoning. The following example demonstrates the point rather well.

> "The scientific magazine *Discover* put the situation this way: "Evolution ... is not only under attack by fundamentalist Christians, but is also being questioned by reputable scientists. Among paleontologists, scientists who study the fossil record, there is growing dissent from the prevailing view of Darwinism.""
> - *Life – How Did it Get Here?* p.15.

The original quote in context reads quite differently.

> "Charles Darwin's brilliant theory of evolution, published in 1859, had a stunning impact on scientific and religious thought and forever changed man's perception of himself. Now that hallowed theory is not only under attack by fundamentalist Christians, but is also being questioned by reputable scientists. Among paleontologists, scientists who study the fossil record, there is growing dissent from the prevailing view of Darwinism.... **Most of the debate will center on one key question: Does the three-billion-year-old process of evolution creep at a steady pace, or is it marked by long periods of inactivity punctuated by short bursts of rapid change? Is Evolution a tortoise or a hare?** Darwin's widely accepted view -- that evolution proceeds steadily, at a crawl -- favors the tortoise. But two paleontologists, Niles Eldredge of the American Museum of Natural History and Stephen Jay Gould of Harvard, are putting their bets on the hare."
> - *"The Tortoise or the Hare?"* Discover, October 1980, p.88.

The above is just one example of a multitude of misleading and incorrect use of quotes by the Watchtower Society. In addition the Society has once again used questionable and possibly occult sources. Francis Hitching was cited thirteen times in the book. Hitching is a paranormalist and has no scientific credentials whatsoever. The book has also been criticised for implying that 'chance' is the only alternative to intelligent design. The reality is that chance, filtered through 'Natural Selection' is the driving force behind evolutionary change.

In 1998, the 'Life' book was replaced by 'Is There a Creator Who Cares About You?' The Society has done a little better in the quote-mining department (though it still has some), but the book contains the same Creationist / Intelligent Design material that organisations like the 'Discovery Institute' produce. Much of the book relies on appealing to the reader's simplistic senses whilst bombarding them with examples of complexity in nature and stating how evolution would be impossible in each case. See 'Appendix E' for a parody example I created.

Repeatedly, the Watchtower Society plays on the incorrect common use meaning of the word 'theory' when referring to the theory of evolution.

> "TODAY, the theory of evolution is said to be a fact by those who promote it." - *Awake!* 8Th June 2000.

> "These statements may be at odds with certain scientific theories, but not with established scientific fact. The history of science shows that theories come and go; the facts remain." - *The Origin of Life – Five Questions Worth Asking.*

Either deliberately or through ignorance the Watchtower Society puts forward the misleading notion that evolution is 'only a theory'. This is however, a typical creationist straw-man argument. For those not in the know, theories in science operate at a higher level than facts. The reason is that theories explain facts. Cell Biologist Professor Ken Miller summarised the misconception as follows:

"Of course it is a theory, but when you say it's a theory, not a fact, you make it sound like theories and facts are opposite things. They're not. Let me put it this way: let's suppose a young person went to university of Georgia to study physics, they have a very good physics department. One of the subjects they have to study is called atomic theory. Now why do we call that atomic theory? Do we call that because we are not really sure about atoms; 'maybe they exists, maybe they don't'? And maybe someday if we get more evidence we can change the name of the subject to atomic facts? Well, the answer is: of course not! We call it atomic theory because what it does is it explains hundreds of thousands of observational and experimental facts about the nature of matter, and that's what theories do. Theories in science don't become facts, theories in science explain facts. Theories are actually a higher level of understanding, and evolutionary theory explains hundreds of thousands of facts and observations about the nature of living things. That's why we call it a theory." - *Ken Miller, speaking at the Chautauqua Institution,* August 18th 2008.

The theory of evolution is the conceptual framework that combines massive bodies of evidence to provide a comprehensive explanation of the diversity of life on the planet. It enables predictions to be made, which when verified add to the mass of evidence already collected. For example, let's take the theory of gravity. The fact is, the apple falls from the tree. The theory of gravity explains the mechanism that causes the apple to fall to the ground. With evolution, the fact is that species are varied and even have the appearance of being designed for a purpose. The best acceptance we get from the Watchtower Society is:

"At best, Darwin's finches show that a species can adapt to changing climates" - *The Origin of Life – Five Questions Worth Asking,* p.21.

However, the theory of evolution explains that species change genetically over time, resulting in physical diversification, speciation and specialisation. Natural Selection filters random mutations, environmental pressures, and more to create animals that are ever more specialised. Mutations that give an advantage to a plant or animal, however small, add to the likelihood that an individual will survive long enough to reproduce, and pass on those same advantages. Once one gains a proper understanding of the theory of evolution, it's power and elegance can be fully appreciated.

The Watchtower Society doesn't stop at mere erroneous definitions however, and has even resorted to some rather outrageous statements.

> "Without doubt, the theory of evolution and false doctrines have contributed to the misery that mankind has experienced during the last days." - *The Watchtower,* 15th May 2013, p.3-7.

> "Therefore, those who put faith in evolution are robbed of true hope." - *The Watchtower,* 15th May 2013, p.3-7.

Surely anyone with just a hint of brainpower can see how fallacious it is to attach the theory of evolution to undefined 'false doctrines' and accuse them of causing much of mankind's misery. No evidence is presented to back up the claim, which adds to its unfounded appearance. Furthermore, to say that people who believe the evidence for evolution are 'robbed of true hope' is quite bizarre. They fail to acknowledge that millions of people who accept evolution also believe in God, and have hope of an afterlife. Also, many who do not accept evolution yet have a religious hope are expected to be destroyed by God at Armageddon for believing in the wrong God. Their hope would also appear to be false from the viewpoint of the Witnesses. The opinion of the Watchtower Society appears to be that the only valid form of hope is an ultimate one. Is it not perfectly reasonable to have a hope to live a long and happy life, and for mankind to improve itself as time goes on? Richard Dawkins brilliantly summed it up:

> "The universe does not owe you a sense of hope. It could be that the world, the universe, is a totally hopeless place. I don't as a

matter of fact think it is, but even if it were - that would not be a good reason for believing in God. You cannot say "I believe in X", whatever X is - God or anything else - "because that gives me hope". You have to say "I believe in X because there is some evidence for X". - *Richard Dawkins, speaking on the BBC programme 'The Big Questions',* 2008.

Does God Exist?

Having left the religion that shaped me through my formative years, I was ever searching for evidence of the existence of God. This included the evidence for design, which as it turns out was pretty much exclusively evidence of the *appearance* of design. There are no discernible 'fingerprints' of a designer, and as physicist Lawrence Krauss has pointed out on numerous occasions, the appearance of design is subjective. Some people see design where others do not. One of the most important recent events in this discussion was the 'Kitzmiller vs. Dover' court case, where the intelligent design 'hypothesis' was on trial, begging for 'equal time' in the classroom alongside the theory of evolution. The result was categorical defeat for the Intelligent Design (ID) community. The conceptual arguments from the ID crowd were exposed to be both heavily flawed and religiously motivated. The sweeping verdict from the highly respected judge (who incidentally is a Christian) ruled that ID was not a legitimate science and it even violated the constitution of the United States.

Why does this matter? The anti-evolution material that the Watchtower Society uses is heavily based on material produced by the ID community. Furthermore, the evidence for the evolutionary history of life on this planet is considerable. The evidence for the existence of God conversely, is minimal.

Learning rational thinking from scientists like Richard Dawkins, PZ Myers, Lawrence Krauss, and commentators like the late Christopher Hitchens has been an awakening. It is clear now how the belief in God was an obvious development as we primitively tried to understand the world around us. Questions like, 'What is that ball of light in the sky?' and, 'What caused my family member to get sick and die?' could at the time only be answered by the presence of a supernatural being/s. A being that is praised for all the good yet is exempt from blame for the bad.

> "I notice when people say, "Look at all we have to be thankful for," or, "Look at what's so wonderful," they mean when the baby falls out of the window and bounced on the soft roof of a car, don't they? They say, "Oh, God had it in his hand." They've nothing to say when the ditches are full of dead babies and no one did a thing.
>
> Look at the beauty of the design of the plague vassilis or the incredible eagerness and hunger and ruthlessness and beauty of the cancer cell or the cobra. Who created all *this*, is what I want to know? If someone wants to take credit for this creation, let them take credit for the whole thing and for all the despair, misery that goes with it. For all the babies that are born without brains at all, or with cancer, or with no chance of living beyond a day. Who's responsible for that? In what mysterious ways does the divinity move when this occurs?" - *Christopher Hitchens.*

Too many questions arise that cannot be answered. If there is a God, how could we know him? Why would there be only one deity? What of all the different God's that have been worshipped throughout history? What was the designer's intention when he gave our sun a lifespan of 10 billion years (of which it is approximately half way through), meaning our days truly are numbered. Why did he create the Andromeda galaxy that's hurtling towards our precious Milky Way, bringing its own promise of destruction along with it? It is not only the concept that the Jehovah's Witnesses have 'The Truth' I contest, but also the concept of any divine existence, that falls apart.

CHAPTER 8

CONCLUSION

My question to you, having stuck with me so far is: what have *you* concluded on the matter? Are you in agreement with my descriptions and analysis of the Jehovah's Witness religion? If you are not, please feel free to write to me and explain your contentions[10]. I feel satisfied that I have portrayed the truth about 'The Truth' in an accurate and concise manner, but will not argue with the fact that the Witnesses have a strong bond of solidarity worldwide. They do engage in a large scale preaching work, and are for the most part honest-hearted individuals who show great love and compassion. They are under the false belief however that they are unique in this way. One of the pleasing discoveries I made was that this love they have is not as unique as I had been told. Rather, there are many more groups of people that actually show more genuine love and not just amongst themselves. These groups are not always religious, and they are not opportunistically recruiting new members in subtle and sly ways. They do not show interest in you as long as you listen to their message and then move on if they

---

[10] info@knockknockbook.co.uk

determine you're not going to join them. There is real, genuine love and kindness in the world. Such must be embraced and furthered for our species to flourish. There are evil and wicked people upon this planet we call home, but they are not everywhere, as the Witnesses would have you believe. Rather than denouncing the world as a lost cause and awaiting divine intervention, it is up to us to make it a better place.

The love that Witnesses show is entirely conditional, despite contrary claims. The 'loving arrangement' to shun former members and treat them as if they do not exist is in fact utterly unloving. The suppression of free thought and expression, the inability to have doubts beyond mere tokens of such, and the bombardment of concentrated information infects and dominates the thinking of the individual. They are left with a distorted view of reality and readily submit to the dictates of a small group of individuals that claim to be directed by God's spirit, yet at the same time state they are not infallible. The individual cuts off all former friendships in favour of their new group of associates. They are slowly isolated from any unbelieving family by means of invisible barriers within their mind. They commit large amounts of time and money in aid of their newly found cause and receive little in return. They follow a belief called 'The Truth' and yet this truth has changed many times, and they accept each change without question. They believe they are part of a chosen few and are in possession of special knowledge. They readily accept whatever they are told by their chosen authority and reject anything that contradicts it. They live the rest of their life in service to an unseen being whilst following the words of men who have no proof of their claims. They die believing they are about to be resurrected to a paradise world, to live in eternal bliss, with no evidence to support this. Yet they feel they have won the battle, having endured to the end.

Finding out the truth about 'The Truth' is the mere beginning of the path to freedom. It is no easy journey, but by learning the **real truth** you can begin to disassemble the 'deeply entrenched things' and begin to formulate your own sense of right and wrong. You will begin to trust your own judgement and build a sense of self-worth that was unattainable in your previous existence.

If you are a Jehovah's Witness who is thinking about leaving, or have some doubts that won't go away[11], you are not the only one. There is a whole support network of former Jehovah's Witnesses that really do care and want to help people who have left or are trying to leave the organisation[12]. Whatever your current situation is or your beliefs are, they are there to listen, support you and offer advice. With their help you will quickly realise there is so much more to life than you had previously thought. Keep talking, keep sharing, and keep FREE!

The Final Word

Since its inception, the Watchtower Society has produced well over two hundred different books for use by its followers. This is in addition to the near countless number of magazines, brochures, tracts, DVDs and audio recordings. Although all but the most recent are considered obsolete due to the many changed teachings. I will let the Bible itself provide the final proverbial 'nail in the coffin', since it is their claimed final authority.

> "To the making of many books there is no end, and much devotion [to them] is wearisome to the flesh" - *Ecclesiastes 12:12, New World Translation.*

Are Jehovah's Witnesses part of a cult? **Without A Doubt!**

Is it worth the effort and pain to get out? **YES!**

---

[11] By reading this book you already have made tremendous progress. Not because it is the answer to all your problems, but because you have crossed a bridge that so few Witnesses would even look at.
[12] One such place I found very helpful is www.jehovahswitnessrecovery.com. The forum is an excellent place to speak to people who really know what it is like to be a Witness, to go through the leaving process, and to come out on the other side.

APPENDIX

A - *Studies in the Scriptures Series III - Thy Kingdom Come* p.342 <u>1891 Edition</u>

342 *Thy Kingdom Come.*

end. The measuring of this period and determining when the pit of trouble shall be reached are easy enough if we have a definite date—a point in the Pyramid from which to start. We have this date-mark in the junction of the "First Ascending Passage" with the "Grand Gallery." That point marks the birth of our Lord Jesus, as the "Well," 33 inches farther on, indicates his death. So, then, if we measure backward down the "First Ascending Passage" to its junction with the "Entrance Passage," we shall have a fixed date to mark upon the downward passage. This measure is 1542 inches, and indicates the year B. C. 1542, as the date at that point. Then measuring *down* the "Entrance Passage" from that point, to find the distance to the entrance of the "Pit," representing the great trouble and destruction with which this age is to close, when evil will be overthrown from power, we find it to be 3416 inches, symbolizing 3416 years from the above date, B. C. 1542. This calculation shows A. D. 1874 as marking the beginning of the period of trouble; for 1542 years B. C. plus 1874 years A. D. equals 3416 years. Thus the Pyramid witnesses that the close of 1874 was the *chronological* beginning of the time of trouble such as was not since there was a nation—no, nor ever shall be afterward. And thus it will be noted that this "Witness" fully corroborates the Bible testimony on this subject, as shown by the "Parallel Dispensations" in MILLENNIAL DAWN, VOL. II., Chap. vii.

Studies in the Scriptures Series III - Thy Kingdom Come p.342 <u>1910 Edition</u>

end. The measuring of this period and determining when the pit of trouble shall be reached are easy enough if we have a definite date—a point in the Pyramid from which to start. We have this date-mark in the junction of the "First Ascending Passage" with the "Grand Gallery." That point marks the birth of our Lord Jesus, as the "Well," 33 inches farther on, indicates his death. So, then, if we measure backward down the "First Ascending Passage" to its junction with the "Entrance Passage," we shall have a fixed date to mark upon the downward passage. This measure is 1542 inches, and indicates the year B. C. 1542, as the date at that point. Then measuring *down* the "Entrance Passage" from that point, to find the distance to the entrance of the "Pit," representing the great trouble and destruction with which this age is to close, when evil will be overthrown from power, we find it to be 3457 inches, symbolizing 3457 years from the above date, B. C. 1542. This calculation shows A. D. 1915 as marking the beginning of the period of trouble; for 1542 years B. C. plus 1915 years A. D. equals 3457 years. Thus the Pyramid witnesses that the close of 1914 will be the beginning of the time of trouble such as was not since there was a nation—no, nor ever shall be afterward. And thus it will be noted that this "Witness" fully corroborates the Bible testimony on this subject, as shown by the "Parallel Dispensations" in SCRIPTURE STUDIES, VOL. II., Chap. vii.

B - Russell's Pyramid Memorial Stone Design (Souvenir Report, Bible Student's Convention 1919)

C - Letter from Dr Mantey to Watchtower Society

"July 11, 1974

Dear Sirs:

I have a copy of your letter addressed to *Caris* in Santa Ana, California, and I am writing to express my disagreement with statements made in that letter, as well as in quotations you have made from the Dana-Mantey Greek Grammar.

(1) Your statement: "their work allows for the rendering found in the Kingdom Interlinear Translation of the Greek Scriptures at John 1:1." There is no statement in our grammar that was ever meant to imply that "a god" was a permissible translation in John 1:1.

A. We had no "rule" to argue in support of the trinity.

B. Neither did we state that we did have such intention. We were simply delineating the facts inherent in Biblical language.

C. You quotation from p. 148 (3) was a paragraph under the heading: "With the subject in a Copulative Sentence." Two examples occur here to illustrate that "the article points out the subject in these examples." But we made no statement in this paragraph about the predicate except that, "as it stands the other persons of the trinity may be implied ;in theos." And isn't that the opposite of what your translation "a god" infers? You quoted me out of context. On pages 139 and 140 (VI) in our grammar we stated: "without the article, *theos* signifies divine essence...'*theos en ho logos*' emphasizes Christ's participation in the essence of the divine nature." Our interpretation is in agreement with that in NEB and TED: "What God was, the Word was"; and with that of Barclay: "The nature of the Word was the same as the nature of God," which you quoted in you letter to Caris.

(2) Since Colwell's and Harner's article in JBL, especially that of Harner, it is neither scholarly nor reasonable to translate John 1:1 "The Word was a god." Word-order has made obsolete and incorrect such a rendering.

(3) Your quotation of Colwell's rule is inadequate because it quotes only a part of his findings. You did not quote this strong assertion: "A predicate nominative which precedes the verb cannot be translated as an indefinite or a 'qualitative' noun solely because of the absence of the article."

(4) Prof. Harner, Vol 92:1 in JBL, has gone beyond Colwell's research and has discovered that anarthrous predicate nouns preceding the verb function primarily to express the nature or character of the subject. He found this true in 53 passages in the Gospel of John and 8 in the Gospel of Mark. Both scholars wrote that when indefiniteness was intended that gospel writers regularly placed the predicate noun after the verb, and both Colwell and Harner have stated that *theos* in John 1:1 is not indefinite and should not be translated "a god." Watchtower writers appear to be the only ones advocating such a translation now. The evidence appears to be 99% against them.

(5) Your statement in your letter that the sacred text itself should guide one and "not just someone's rule book." We agree with you. But our study proves that Jehovah's Witnesses do the opposite of that whenever the "sacred text" differs with their heretical beliefs. For example the translation of *kolasis* as *cutting off* when punishment is the only meaning cited in the lexicons for it. The mistranslation of *ego eimi* as "I have been" in John 8:58, the addition of "for all time" in Heb. 9:27 when nothing in the Greek New Testament support is. The attempt to belittle Christ by mistranslating a*rche tes kriseos* "beginning of the creation" when he is magnified as the "creator of all things" (John 1:2) and as "equal with God" (Phil. 2:6) before he humbled himself and lived a human body on earth. Your quotation of "The father is greater than I am, (John 14:28) to prove that Jesus was not equal to God overlooks the fact stated in Phil 2:6-8.

When Jesus said that he was still in his voluntary state of humiliation. That state ended when he ascended to heaven. Why the attempt to deliberately deceive people by mispunctuation by placing a comma after "today" in Luke 23:43 when in the Greek, Latin, German and all English translations except yours, *even in the Greek in your KIT*, the comma occurs after *lego* (I say) - "Today you will be with me in Paradise." 2 Cor 5:8, "to be out of the body and at home with the Lord."

These passages teach that the redeemed go immediately to heaven after death, which does not agree with your teachings that death ends all life until the resurrection. (Ps. 23:6 and Heb 1:10)

The above are only a few examples of Watchtower mistranslations and perversions of God's Word.

In view of the preceding facts, especially because you have been quoting me out of context, I herewith request you not to quote the *Manual Grammar of the Greek New Testament* again, which you have been doing for 24 years. Also that you not quote it or me in any of your publications from this time on.

Also that you publicly and immediately apologize in the Watchtower magazine, since my words had no relevance to the absence of the article before *theos* in John 1:1. And please write to Caris and state that you misused and misquoted my "rule."

On the page before the *Preface* in the grammar are these words: "All rights reserved - no part of this book may be reproduced in any form without permission in writing from the publisher."

If you have such permission, please send me a photo-copy of it.

If you do not heed these requests you will suffer the consequences.

Regretfully yours,

Julius R. Mantey"

D - Letter from United Nations

DEPARTMENT OF PUBLIC INFORMATION

DPI ⬥ NGO

NON-GOVERNMENTAL ORGANIZATIONS SECTION

United Nations, DPI/NGO Resource Centre, Room L-1B-31
Tel: (212) 963-7233, 7234, 7078 • Fax: (212) 963-2819 • E-mail: dpingo@un.org

4 March 2004

To Whom It May Concern,

Recently the NGO Section has been receiving numerous inquiries regarding the association of the **Watchtower Bible and Tract Society of New York** with the Department of Public Information (DPI). This organization applied for association with DPI in 1991 and was granted association in 1992. By accepting association with DPI, the organization agreed to meet criteria for association, including support and respect of the principles of the Charter of the United Nations and commitment and means to conduct effective information programmes with its constituents and to a broader audience about UN activities.

In October 2001, the Main Representative of the **Watchtower Bible and Tract Society of New York** to the United Nations, Giro Aulicino, requested termination of its association with DPI. Following this request, the DPI made a decision to disassociate the **Watchtower Bible and Tract Society of New York** as of 9 October 2001.

Please be informed that it is the policy of the Department of Public Information of the United Nations to keep correspondence between the United Nations and NGOs associated with DPI confidential. However, please see below the paragraph included in all letters sent to NGOs approved for association in 1992:

"The principal purpose of association of non-governmental organizations with the United Nations Department of Public Information is the redissemination of information in order to increase public understanding of the principles, activities and achievements of the United Nations and its Agencies. Consequently, it is important that you should keep us informed about your organization's information programme as it relates to the United Nations, including sending us issues of your relevant publications. We are enclosing a brochure on the "The United Nations and Non-Governmental Organizations", which will give you some information regarding the NGO relationship."

In addition, the criteria for NGOs to become associated with DPI include the following:
- that the NGO share the principles of the UN Charter;
- operate solely on a not-for-profit basis;
- have a demonstrated interest in United Nations issues and a proven ability to reach large or specialized audiences, such as educators, media representatives, policy makers and the business community;

- have the commitment and means to conduct effective information programmes about UN activities by publishing newsletters, bulletins and pamphlets, organizing conferences, seminars and round tables; and enlisting the cooperation of the media.

We expect that you will share this information with your concerned colleagues, as we are unable to address the scores of duplicate requests regarding the Watchtower Bible and Tract Society that are being directed to our offices. Thank you for your interest in the work of the United Nations.

Sincerely,

Paul Hoeffel
Chief
NGO Section
Department of Public Information

E - Parody Of Awake! Magazine's 'Was It Designed' Series

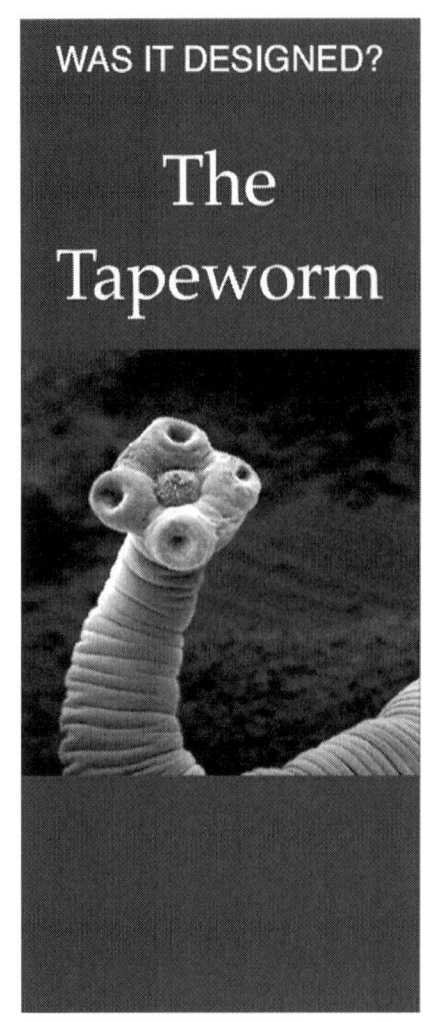

WAS IT DESIGNED?

The Tapeworm

- The tapeworm can live inside a human for as long as 20 years, and grow to 50 feet long.

Consider: Scientists claim this creature to be a parasite, yet they marvel at the simple life it leads.

With it's gentle nature and quiet complexion, the human loving tapeworm resides in your intestines often causing little or no symptoms.

Many christians would do well to remember that our loving God never wants us to feel alone, and with a loving tapeworm inside us, we need not.*

Doesn't it warm your heart and strengthen your faith to know that our loving creator has gone to such lengths to provide for every need we may ever have...?

What do you think? Did the tapeworm come about by chance? Or was it designed?

*Some christians believe that God allowed man to eat meat so he would be able to benefit from the company of tapeworms. Doesn't it testify to the foresight our loving creator has?

F - Letter from Watchtower Headquarters to All Congregation Elders – Ref: Shepherd the Flock of God book

Christian Congregation of Jehovah's Witnesses

2821 Route 22, Patterson, NY 12563-2237   Phone: (845) 306-1100

August 23, 2010

TO ALL BODIES OF ELDERS

Re: Kingdom Ministry School

Dear Brothers:

Final arrangements are being made for the upcoming Kingdom Ministry School, and we are now pleased to provide you with some additional information and direction.

A revised, softcover textbook entitled *"Shepherd the Flock of God"—1 Peter 5:2* has been prepared in connection with the school. In addition, lapel cards are being provided for elders and ministerial servants for use as identification upon entry at the school location and during the course. The appropriate number of textbooks will be shipped to the mailing address of the coordinator of the body of elders when the textbooks become available in the language of the congregation. The lapel cards will be shipped to the same address at a later date. Copies of the textbook that were requested in languages other than the language of the congregation will be sent to the circuit overseer for distribution.

The coordinator of the body of elders should immediately give each elder a copy of the *Shepherding* textbook. However, the lapel cards should be kept in a safe place until the week before the school. Then he should give the appropriate card to each elder and ministerial servant. This may prevent cards from being lost. The lapel card should be worn when entering the school location and at all times during the school. We will leave it to each elder to decide what he will do with his 1991 Kingdom Ministry School textbook. If he decides to keep the book, he must make sure it is put in a secure place so that others do not have access to it. Otherwise, the book should be completely destroyed.

We would like to emphasize the importance of keeping these new textbooks secured and confidential, both before and after they are distributed. The textbooks should not be left on tops of desks or in other places where they are easily accessible by family members or other individuals. The information is designed for use by the **elders only**, and other individuals should not have any opportunity to read the information.

If an elder has moved away and you have an extra textbook or lapel card, or for some other reason you have extra textbooks or lapel cards, the coordinator of the body of elders should hand-deliver them to the circuit overseer. He should not send textbooks or lapel cards through the mail. If your circuit overseer is a considerable distance away, the coordinator of the body of elders may give him these items the next time he sees the circuit overseer. Likewise, if for some reason you do not receive enough textbooks or lapel cards, the coordinator of the body of elders should contact the circuit overseer for assistance.

We are providing the textbooks to elders in advance so that you will be able to read the book through before attending the school. You will want to concentrate particularly on chapters 1, 2, 4-7, 9, and 11, since they will be considered specifically at the school. In addition to your *Shepherding* textbook, please remember to bring your Bible, *Organized to Do Jehovah's Will*, *Benefit From Theocratic Ministry School Education*, and some note paper. In the *Organized* book, you should review chapters 3 and 7, along with pages 117-119. In the *Ministry School*

Re: Kingdom Ministry School
August 23, 2010
Page 2

book, you should review pages 47-55, 130, and 265-271. Please advise ministerial servants that in addition to their Bible and note paper, they should bring their *Organized* and *Ministry School* books. They should review the same material in the *Ministry School* book as the elders, and in the *Organized* book, they should review chapters 6-8, along with pages 117-119.

You will note in chapter 5, paragraph 9, of the *Shepherding* textbook that a change in terminology is being introduced. A new term, "brazen conduct," will be used in addition to "loose conduct," or in some cases instead of "loose conduct." This new term has been chosen by the Governing Body because it more accurately conveys the thought of the original Greek word that is translated "loose conduct" in the *New World Translation*.

The Governing Body desires that elders and ministerial servants in each congregation attend the school at the same time. However, if an appointed elder or ministerial servant is not able to attend with the elders and ministerial servants of his congregation because of extenuating circumstances, he can contact his circuit overseer for the dates and locations of schools in neighboring circuits. The circuit overseer will then contact the neighboring circuit overseer and request permission for the brother to attend. The brother's coordinator of the body of elders should provide him with a lapel card. If he attends the school before other elders or ministerial servants in his congregation, he should be instructed to keep the information strictly confidential until after the other brothers from his congregation have attended.

Any brother appointed as an elder or ministerial servant in his congregation may attend the school. If new appointments are made, the coordinator of the body of elders should inform the circuit overseer of this so that the brother can receive the appropriate lapel card, and a new *Shepherding* textbook if he is being appointed as an elder. If an elder or ministerial servant is in the process of transferring from one congregation to another and comes with a favorable recommendation from his former congregation, and if the circuit overseer has not yet served his new congregation since his move, then the circuit overseer should provide him with a lapel card. If the circuit overseer has served the new congregation and the brother has been recommended for appointment to the branch office, then the circuit overseer would also provide him with a card. However, if the circuit overseer has visited the new congregation since the brother moved in and the body of elders did not recommend his reappointment for some reason, then he should not attend the school.

We are looking forward to this special program of instruction, and we pray for Jehovah's rich blessing upon all the arrangements being made for the Kingdom Ministry School and upon your efforts to shepherd the flock in a fine way. Although there is much material to prepare before attending the school, the most important thing to prepare is your heart. (Ezra 7:10) If you do so, Jehovah will truly bless your diligent efforts. Please be assured of our warm love and Christian greetings.

Your brothers,

*Christian Congregation
of Jehovah's Witnesses*

cc: Traveling overseers

PS to secretary:

There is no need for this letter to be retained in the congregation permanent file of policy letters. Additionally, the September 16, 1991, and June 20, 1994, letters to all bodies of elders should be removed from the congregation file and be destroyed. You may wish to update the congregation copy of *Index to Letters—For Bodies of Elders* (S-22) at this time as well.

G - Letter from Watchtower Headquarters to All Congregation Elders – Ref: Binding of the Shepherd the Flock of God book

Christian Congregation of Jehovah's Witnesses

2821 Route 22, Patterson, NY 12563-2237 Phone: (845) 306-1100

October 7, 2010

TO ALL BODIES OF ELDERS

Re: Spiral binding of *Shepherding* textbook

Dear Brothers:

Since the release of the new *Shepherding* textbook, several elders have asked about the possibility of having their textbook spiral bound. There is no objection if an elder personally spiral binds or laminates his own textbook or does so for other elders. If he has another baptized brother who is not an elder do the work for him, the elder must watch while the work is being done. Outside companies, unbelievers, or sisters are not permitted to do this work. The material in the book is confidential, and confidentiality must be preserved.

Each elder should make the following notation next to the box on the title page of the *Shepherding* textbook: "See letter dated October 7, 2010, to all bodies of elders regarding spiral binding of this textbook."

Please be assured of our warm Christian love and best wishes.

Your brothers,
*Christian Congregation
of Jehovah's Witnesses*

cc: Traveling overseers

PS to secretary:

This letter should be retained in the congregation permanent file of policy letters. You may wish to update the congregation copy of *Index to Letters—For Bodies of Elders* (S-22) at this time as well.

RECOMMENDED READING

Web
http://www.carm.org/jehovahs-witnesses
http://www.forananswer.org/Top_JW/Scholars%20and%20NWT.htm
http://www.guardian.co.uk/uk/2001/oct/08/religion.world
http://www.guardian.co.uk/uk/2001/oct/15/religion.unitednations?INTCMP=SRCH
http://www.jehovahswitnessrecovery.com
http://www.jwfacts.com
http://www.richarddawkins.net
http://www.talkorigins.org

Books
-Cameron, Don. Captives of a Concept. Lulu Inc, 2006.
-Coyne, J. *Why Evolution is True*. Oxford University Press, 2010.
-Dawkins, R. *The God Delusion*. Transworld Publishers, 2007.
-Dawkins, R. *The Greatest Show on Earth*. Edition, 2010.
-Franz, R. *Crisis of Conscience*. Commentary Press, 1983.
-Greer, J. M. *Apocalypse*. Quercus, 2012.
-Harris, S. *Letter to a Christian Nation*. Transworld Publishers, 2007.
-Harris, S. *The End of Faith*. The Free Press, 2005.
-Hassan, S. Combatting Cult Mind Control. Park Street Press, 1990.
-Hitchens, C. *God is Not Great*. Atlantic Books, 2007.

REFERENCES

Chapter 1
- Undisclosed Author(s). *Awake!*. Watchtower Bible & Tract Society, 2011 (November).
-Undisclosed Author(s). *Jehovah's Witnesses Annual Report*. Watchtower Bible & Tract Society, 2012.
-Undisclosed Author(s). *New World Translation of the Holy Scriptures*. Watchtower Bible & Tract Society, 1984.
-Undisclosed Author(s). *Questions Young People Ask: Vol II*. Watchtower Bible & Tract Society, 2008.
-Undisclosed Author(s). *Reasoning from the Scriptures*. Watchtower Bible & Tract Society, 1989.
-Undisclosed Author(s). *Revelation, Its Grand Climax at Hand!* Watchtower Bible & Tract Society, 1988 (revised) 2006).
-Undisclosed Author(s). *The Greatest Name*. Watchtower Bible & Tract Society, 1994 (revised 2001).
-Undisclosed Author(s). *The Watchtower*. Watchtower Bible & Tract Society, 1951 (February 1st).
-Undisclosed Author(s). *The Watchtower*. Watchtower Bible & Tract Society, 1982 (February 15th).
-Undisclosed Author(s). *The Watchtower*. Watchtower Bible & Tract Society, 1989 (September 1st).
-Undisclosed Author(s). *The Watchtower*. Watchtower Bible & Tract Society, 1993 (October 1st).
-Undisclosed Author(s). *The Watchtower*. Watchtower Bible & Tract Society, 1994 (February 15th).
-Undisclosed Author(s). *The Watchtower*. Watchtower Bible & Tract Society, 1995 (February 15th).
-Undisclosed Author(s). *The Watchtower*. Watchtower Bible & Tract Society, 2000 (January 15th).
-Undisclosed Author(s). *The Watchtower*. Watchtower Bible & Tract Society, 2002 (July 15th).
-Undisclosed Author(s). *The Watchtower*. Watchtower Bible & Tract Society, 2007 (January 15th).
-Undisclosed Author(s). *The Watchtower*. Watchtower Bible & Tract Society, 2007 (October 1st).
-Undisclosed Author(s). *The Watchtower*. Watchtower Bible & Tract

Society, 2013 (January 15th).
-Undisclosed Author(s). *What Does The Bible Really Teach?* Watchtower Bible & Tract Society, 2006.

Chapter 2
-Undisclosed Author(s). *Organized to Do Jehovah's Will.* Watchtower Bible & Tract Society, 2005.

Chapter 3
-Undisclosed Author(s). *The Watchtower.* Watchtower Bible & Tract Society, 2009 (November 15th).

Chapter 4
-Undisclosed Author(s). *Awake!.* Watchtower Bible & Tract Society, 2009 (July).
-Undisclosed Author(s). *New World Translation of the Holy Scriptures.* Watchtower Bible & Tract Society, 1984.

Chapter 5
-Cameron, Don. Captives of a Concept. Lulu Inc, 2006.
-Russell, C. T. *Studies in the Scriptures III - Thy Kingdom Come.* Watchtower Bible & Tract Society, 1908.
-Russell, C. T. *Studies in the Scriptures III - Thy Kingdom Come.* Watchtower Bible & Tract Society, 1910.
-Russell, C. T. *Studies in the Scriptures III - Thy Kingdom Come.* Watchtower Bible & Tract Society, 1915.
-Russell, C. T. *Studies in the Scriptures I - The Divine Plan of the Ages.* Zion's Watchtower Tract Society, 1886.
-Russell, C. T. *Thy Kingdom Come.* Zion's Watchtower Tract Society, 1891.
-Rutherford, J. F. *The Finished Mystery.* Watchtower Bible & Tract Society, 1917.
-Undisclosed Author(s). *Awake!* Watchtower Bible & Tract Society, 1968 (October 8th).
-Undisclosed Author(s). *Awake!* Watchtower Bible & Tract Society, 1969 (May 22nd).
-Undisclosed Author(s). *Awake!* Watchtower Bible & Tract Society, 1993

(August 8th).
-Undisclosed Author(s). *Jehovah's Witnesses - Proclaimers of God's Kingdom.* Watchtower Bible & Tract Society, 1993.
-Undisclosed Author(s). *Kingdom Ministry.* Watchtower Bible & Tract Society, 1947 (May).
-Undisclosed Author(s). *Pastor Russell's Convention Discourses.* Unknown Publisher, 1916.
-Undisclosed Author(s). *Revelation, Its Grand Climax at Hand!* Watchtower Bible & Tract Society, 1988 (revised) 2006).
-Undisclosed Author(s). *The Golden Age.* Watchtower Bible & Tract Society, 1921 (October 12th).
-Undisclosed Author(s). *The Golden Age.* Watchtower Bible & Tract Society, 1926 (April 7th).
-Undisclosed Author(s). *The Golden Age.* Watchtower Bible & Tract Society, 1929 (November 12th).
-Undisclosed Author(s). *The Truth That Leads to Eternal Life.* Watchtower Bible & Tract Society, 1968.
-Undisclosed Author(s). *The Truth That Leads to Eternal Life.* Watchtower Bible & Tract Society, 1981.
-Undisclosed Author(s). *The Watchtower.* Watchtower Bible & Tract Society, 1925 (May 15th).
-Undisclosed Author(s). *The Watchtower.* Watchtower Bible & Tract Society, 1947 (December 15th).
-Undisclosed Author(s). *The Watchtower.* Watchtower Bible & Tract Society, 1955 (October 1st).
-Undisclosed Author(s). *The Watchtower.* Watchtower Bible & Tract Society, 1967 (November 15th).
-Undisclosed Author(s). *The Watchtower.* Watchtower Bible & Tract Society, 1968 (May 1st).
-Undisclosed Author(s). *The Watchtower.* Watchtower Bible & Tract Society, 1974 (December 15th).
-Undisclosed Author(s). *The Watchtower.* Watchtower Bible & Tract Society, 1975 (May 1st).
-Undisclosed Author(s). *The Watchtower.* Watchtower Bible & Tract Society, 1976 (July 15th).
-Undisclosed Author(s). *The Watchtower.* Watchtower Bible & Tract Society, 1979 (January 1st).
-Undisclosed Author(s). *The Watchtower.* Watchtower Bible & Tract

Society, 1980 (March 15th).
-Undisclosed Author(s). *The Watchtower.* Watchtower Bible & Tract Society, 1983 (April 1st).
-Undisclosed Author(s). *The Watchtower.* Watchtower Bible & Tract Society, 1984 (September 1st).
-Undisclosed Author(s). *The Watchtower.* Watchtower Bible & Tract Society, 1987 (September 1st).
-Undisclosed Author(s). *The Watchtower.* Zion's Watchtower Tract Society, 1894 (July 15th).
-Undisclosed Author(s). *What Does The Bible Really Teach?* Watchtower Bible & Tract Society, 2006.

Chapter 6
-Hassan, S. Combatting Cult Mind Control. Park Street Press, 1990.
-Undisclosed Author(s). *Insight on the Scriptures: Vol II.* Watchtower Bible & Tract Society, 1988.
-Undisclosed Author(s). *The Watchtower.* Watchtower Bible & Tract Society, 1967 (June 1st).
-Undisclosed Author(s). *The Watchtower.* Watchtower Bible & Tract Society, 2006 (February 15th).
-Undisclosed Author(s). *The Watchtower.* Watchtower Bible & Tract Society, 2008 (April 15th).
-Undisclosed Author(s). *The Watchtower.* Watchtower Bible & Tract Society, 2009 (February 15th).
-Undisclosed Author(s). *The Watchtower.* Watchtower Bible & Tract Society, 2010 (January 15th).
-Undisclosed Author(s). *The Watchtower.* Watchtower Bible & Tract Society, 2011 (July 15th).
-Undisclosed Author(s). *The Watchtower.* Watchtower Bible & Tract Society, 2012 (April 15th).

Chapter 7
-Dawkins, R. *The God Delusion.* Transworld Publishers, 2007.
-Franz, R. *Crisis of Conscience.* Commentary Press, 1983.
-Gorman, J. *The Tortoise or the Hare.* Discover, 1980 (October).
-Undisclosed Author(s). *Awake!* Watchtower Bible & Tract Society, 2000 (June 8th).

-Undisclosed Author(s). *Awake!* Watchtower Bible & Tract Society, 2006 (September).
-Undisclosed Author(s). *Letter to All Bodies of Elders.* Watchtower Bible & Tract Society, 2010 (August 23rd).
-Undisclosed Author(s). *Letter to All Bodies of Elders.* Watchtower Bible & Tract Society, 2010 (October 7th).
-Undisclosed Author(s). *Life - Five Questions Worth Asking.* Watchtower Bible & Tract Society, 2006 (September).
-Undisclosed Author(s). *Life - How Did it Get Here?* Watchtower Bible & Tract Society, 1985.
-Undisclosed Author(s). *New World Translation of the Holy Scriptures.* Watchtower Bible & Tract Society, 1984.
-Undisclosed Author(s). *Reasoning from the Scriptures.* Watchtower Bible & Tract Society, 1989.
-Undisclosed Author(s). *Shepherd the Flock of God.* Watchtower Bible & Tract Society, 2010.
-Undisclosed Author(s). *The Watchtower.* Watchtower Bible & Tract Society, 1931 (November 1st).
-Undisclosed Author(s). *The Watchtower.* Watchtower Bible & Tract Society, 1973 (July 1st).
-Undisclosed Author(s). *The Watchtower.* Watchtower Bible & Tract Society, 1994 (October 1st).
-Undisclosed Author(s). *The Watchtower.* Watchtower Bible & Tract Society, 2007 (May 1st).
-Undisclosed Author(s). *The Watchtower.* Watchtower Bible & Tract Society, 2012 (May 15th).
-Undisclosed Author(s). *The Watchtower.* Watchtower Bible & Tract Society, 2013 (May 15th).
-Undisclosed Author(s). *What Does The Bible Really Teach?* Watchtower Bible & Tract Society, 2006.

Chapter 8

-Undisclosed Author(s). *New World Translation of the Holy Scriptures.* Watchtower Bible & Tract Society, 1984.

Printed in Great Britain
by Amazon